Speaking Together

Speaking Together

Canada's Native Women

 Secretary
of State

Secrétariat
d'État

D.S.S. CONTRACT No. 07KX-41411-6-2087
PRINTED AND BOUND BY THE HUNTER ROSE COMPANY, TORONTO
CATALOGUE No. CIT-20E

Ottawa, Canada
1975

Table of Contents

5

Preface

I am pleased to introduce *Speaking Together,* a publication outlining the involvement and achievements of native women across Canada.

My department has always been deeply concerned with Canada's native people, and particularly with native women. The establishment of a special program for native women, and the publication of *Speaking Together* are reflections of that concern.

The women of *Speaking Together* have made significant contributions to Canadian society. Through this series of biographies and personal views, we can understand and share their achievements, concerns and aspirations.

The Hon. J. Hugh Faulkner
Secretary of State

Introduction

9

The idea for a book by and for native women in Canada came to mind as plans were being drawn up for International Women's Year. It grew from our awareness that to be a woman is difficult but to be a woman and a descendant of the first inhabitants of this continent doubles the dilemma that we, as native women, are facing in today's society.

From diverse linguistic and cultural affiliations and from different geographic areas, several native women were chosen to express their views, opinions and experiences of a society that has dramatically changed the life style of our people within a few generations.

Many of you were approached. Some of you were not able to participate and unfortunately, due to the lack of space and time, many of you who were interviewed could not be included in this book. With the help of an advisory group of native women, a selection was made on the basis of background, age, occupation, interests and geographic area.

As native women, your achievements are substantial. Aware and concerned about an impending loss of our vital and viable culture, you have endeavoured to create positive achievements and images, not only for yourself but for our people as well. You are to be commended for maintaining a strong base for your cultural values and for the family unit, at a time when many of our people were experiencing the bitter realities of a changing society with all its implications and supposed benefits. Each of you, through your involvement and combined efforts, has shared a common purpose – that of helping others.

Speaking Together is a collective expression of the concerns, thoughts and aspirations that you hold for future generations of Canadian native people.

For the non-native reader, these biographies express an alternative approach to life from the original inhabitants of this land.

Jean Goodwill
Coordinator
Native Women's Program

Pacific Coast
and Interior

11

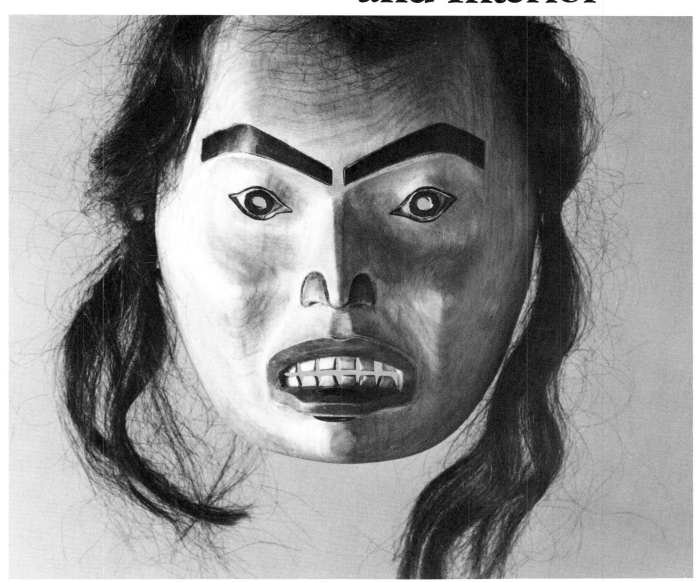

Marjorie Cantryn

people in various capacities ever since. For the past four years she has held the position of Executive Director of the Vancouver Indian Centre Society.

I spent 11 years at residential schools and missed growing up with my brothers but I guess it helped me to adjust to city life. The school principal was like my guardian. I was with him more than my own parents. When I was leaving school he was worried about discrimination and advised me not to work in an office where there would only be a few other Indian girls but to be a nurse because there were lots of ethnic groups working in hospitals. I never regretted that training. It gave me a chance to work with people, especially my own people. When I moved to the city I experienced a lot of things students go through, loneliness, no place to go and nothing to do with free time. I married a non-Indian but he knew how I felt about Indian people and really encouraged me in my work to help my people. I joined a small group operating as the Coqualeetza Fellowship and at 23 years old I became their youngest president. I spent the next year speaking to various service groups, trying to make the public aware of Indian people, how we were trying to integrate into their society and that the success of our integration depended as much on them as it did on ourselves.

Our Friendship Centre was successful because it started at the grass roots level so no one could say "they" are trying to organize us. There is a resentment when people are not ready for things they are asked to do. I have been involved with Friendship Centres ever since and have been

Marjorie Cantryn, a former member of the Ohiet Band at Bamfield, British Columbia, was born in Port Alberni on Vancouver Island. Her forefathers were hereditary Chiefs of the Tseshat, Ucleuelet, Port Alberni and Ohiet Bands. In 1955, she was the first Indian from her area to leave the reserve to pursue an education and a trade. She succeeded by graduating as a practical nurse the following year and has worked among her

13 president of the provincial association and secretary and vice-president of the national association. During this time I got acquainted with agencies in the city, many of them related to court counselling services. This led to my interest in working with ex-inmates and I became the founding president of the Allied Indian and Metis Society, setting up a half-way house for Indian ex-inmates. I was also the first woman to sit on the Vancouver Police Commissioner's Board. Aside from this work I am a board member of the B.C. Association of Non-Status Indians.

When I got married I was told to sign a piece of paper, so I did. Then I got a blue card saying I was no longer a band member nor recognized as an Indian by the Government of Canada. That really shakes you up. I am more aware of my Indianness today than when I was a registered Indian simply because I understand the situation more. That blue card! If I could tear it up and burn it I would.

Today I think society is more aware of Indian people due to their migration into cities. We have quite a number of successful Indians in Canada and native women are becoming more involved than ever before. In the future we will eventually become independent and self-sufficient. Cultural identity seems more important while you are in the city. I notice this especially among students. A year ago my husband and I put on a Potlach to introduce our two daughters to their people in a traditional manner. It was a way of saying: "Girls, these are my people and I want you to know them. Even though you are away you are still with them." Leaving the reserve does not mean we lose contact with our people.

Rose Charlie

Rose Charlie was born on the Chehalis reserve near Vancouver but spent many school years in the United States. After marriage she moved back to Canada and started working for the reserve. When the Homemakers Clubs in British Columbia formed a group, she was elected as head. More recently she was appointed to the British Columbia Human Rights Commission.

Since women are so directly involved with the poverty cycle our people are now in, they are the ones who know what the needs are and can do something. Men are often away working and don't always know what the women have to put up with at home: illness, no water system, overcrowding. So many of our people are down in the gutter because they feel that's the only place for them – but it's not.

When we moved back here there was hardly anything going on. The nearest city was 30 miles away and there was only a narrow gravel road from Chehalis to the main highway. Few families had a car so they were unable to take their children out on educational trips or just sightseeing.

I asked my husband if he'd object if I got the women together to see what we could do, maybe raise money for something, a community hall or whatever people wanted. He said it was up to me so I wrote notes inviting all the women to a meeting in my house and they all turned out, every one of them. I didn't know them all so I told them we could get acquainted and maybe do something for the kids. These women had never been at a meeting before, not even a band council.

We put a saucer in the middle of the table and all put in a nickel. That was the start of our fund raising 23 years ago. We had dances, bingo games and cake sales and within a year we proudly banked $500 once or twice a month for activities such as children's May Day and other special occasions. Our first accomplishment was a new church. That's what people wanted.

15   Then we met with other Homemakers Clubs and had a rally to form a provincial body. At present we have 93 native women's groups in B.C. Sometime I hope to see clubs in all 188 bands in the province.

We get called so often for help by chiefs and councillors. They ask us to come in and organize the women of the community. But often we don't have the money to go. Our office would have closed a few years ago if we hadn't got a grant for leadership training from the Anglican Church's Relief Fund. It was surprising what the women learned on that program, just to know they had rights and could get up and say what they wanted.

In Vancouver we have established a clothing depot for needy and burned-out families. B.C. Telephone Company and Northwest Shipping take clothes free of charge for us when their trucks and ships go to outlying places. They've helped a lot.

Recently we have opened an arts and crafts store in a hotel shopping mall. When we asked government for funds they said to come back when we had a manageress to run it. Then we had to negotiate for six months without funds ourselves for final status of a grant and a loan. It was hard but this did mean some employment for our people. After three years of hard work on the reserve level throughout the province, we were not giving up till we accomplished our goal. Now people are beginning to see what can be done, with pride and determination, in striving for our people.

Hattie Fergusson

Hattie Fergusson of the Tsimshian tribe was born at Hazelton in northern British Columbia in 1908. She is a member of the Eagle clan (with the Indian name Asp-u-ah, meaning "wherever the Sun Shines", representing the Sun Spirit) and its associate medicine clan, the Frog clan (with the name Ksim-hi-wis, meaning the "Woman of mist and rain"). She was educated at Coqualeetza Indian residential school and Chilliwack High School. Years later, she and other graduates formed the Coqualeetza Fellowship, a group which originated the concept of Indian friendship centres to help Indian students become oriented to urban life. Hattie is director of the newly-formed Northwest Indian Cultural Society. She is working as its organizer and promoter and lives in Vancouver.

My tribe is a matriarchal society and the boss was always a woman. Men were the secondary chiefs. The oldest girl is always the head chieftainess in any family and I was the oldest. My totem has three figures. The top is the eagle and underneath it is a frog, symbol of the medicine people. Each main clan has a medicine clan associated with it. Halfway down the pole is the raven which shows my grandmother's relationship to Haida people. Way back in history the tribes were strictly separated and the Haidas were all ravens, but now they have eagle people over on the Queen Charlotte Islands.

The old chieftain classes were broken up when government started to meddle. They selected someone four ranks below my father as chief and that hurt his pride badly. I'm very proud of him. He was an Indian who educated himself pretty well, spoke English and learned to read and write, and adapted himself to white man's ways though he still retained Tsimshian traditions in our home. He was a member of the Fireweed clan, earth people, the historians of the tribe. He went to every reserve where we moved to learn the history of the people. I spent a lot of time with him.

When I finished school and went around looking for work in Vancouver, I found that Indians were not very welcome in those days so I had quite a rough time. After I married, I had a lot of time on my hands. Then one day someone I had known at school came to talk about establishing an Indian centre for youth coming into town as strangers with no place to go. I was very much against it at first as I thought it would be creating another reserve in the city but I changed my mind. We had a grandiose plan for really palatial Indian centres and we put on dances and bazaars and did all sorts of things to collect money. Then

17   Winnipeg wrote to us and we sent them our plan and their centre was going before ours. It took 14 years before we could talk people in Vancouver into it.

After we started the centre the Coqualeetza Fellowship disbanded, thinking the centre would run itself. I think that was a mistake. The centre has deviated from what it was going to do. The thing that needs improvement there is the youth activities. I think they've fallen down on that but I haven't been there for a bit so maybe I'm misjudging them. I helped them organize then figured it was time they paddled their own canoe. The new B.C. government appointed me to Vancouver Community College Board. I was as green as grass – the first Indian. When an Indian is thrown into something new it is really tough. You're not too sure of yourself.

I've been with the Northwest Indian Cultural Society all the time, sitting in on the preliminary meetings before it was formed. Its purpose is to create a better understanding between Indians and non-Indians of the cultural and philosophical aspects of Indian tribal lifestyles. We display Indian arts, put on shows of dancing and give lectures, and we want to form an Indian village to create jobs for native people. We finally got some money and a group together and have called it the Northwest Silk Screening Enterprises. Next we're going to incorporate silverwork and woodwork. It's going to expand we hope. The next thing I have my eye on is the handicapped. I think we can work them into the crafts. There are an awful lot of handicapped native people and nobody pays any attention to them.

Mildred Gottfriedson

In 1964, Mildred Gottfriedson of the Salish-Shuswap tribe, Kamloops, B.C. won the Mother-of-the-Year award for her extensive involvement in community activities. Mrs. Gottfriedson has raised 12 of her own children as well as being a foster parent to many others. Working primarily with native women's groups and children, her main objective has always been the revival of her tribal culture through language training, crafts and traditional dancing.

Back in 1948, living conditions among our people in the interior of British Columbia were deteriorating, especially in housing. The fact that the water system was bad and that there was no plumbing caused a real concern among the women who had to look after their homes and children. Two years later the Homemakers Clubs were forming throughout B.C. and it seemed that the ladies had become more aggressive in expressing the needs of their communities.

Since activities for youth on the reserve, especially for young girls, were lacking, I started a softball club. The first, for the little ones, we called the Pony Tail Club. Then we started one for juniors and finally senior women. Eventually we joined the city league of Kamloops and became involved in city sports events.

In 1960, discrimation towards Indian people was becoming more evident. There were certain restaurants that did not allow our people in so some of us formed a group called the Mika Nika Club which means "You and I" in our language. It was a mixed organization of Indians and non-Indians. We involved lawyers, doctors, RCMP and the general public. One of our founding and most active members was Len Marchand who is now a federal member of Parliament. We dealt with many issues but primarily unemployment which we felt was due to the discrimination that existed in the city. It was during these years that I was chosen Good Citizen of Kamloops & District. Then I became provincial Mother-of-the-Year and then attended the national contest.

The following years I became involved in the North American Indian Brotherhood, an organization that included both men and women. We worked on the land claims issues, towards integrated schools and getting liquor rights for our people. The B.C. Native Women's Society then came into being with similar objectives as the Homemakers Clubs in B.C. It seemed that it was always the women who took a greater interest in the home conditions and who were capable of presenting their views and concerns to government agencies.

From there on, I became more involved outside the province as a member of the National Education Committee and the National Indian Cultural Committee. This took a lot of travelling and kept me away from home but it gave me a greater outlook on what other native people were doing in other provinces.

19   I am now back to working at the community level where the greatest needs are. At the reserve level we are implementing programs to bring in social aide-workers, teachers' aides and community health workers. The women are still the strongest force behind these programs. We believe that our people have to be trained first in these areas, particularly in the administration of their own band affairs. Some men do reject the idea of women taking leadership roles but we feel that it's our responsibility. It is the woman who is always present from the time she carries and bears her child, to the time that child goes to school and brings home his or her problems. It's the mother who talks to the teacher, takes the child to the doctor when necessary, etc. We tell our men we want to be involved in all these negotiations that are taking place since we are the ones who are affected by any policy changes in the future.

I think that if we had more information from outside sources we would be more involved. Of course, my main concern is the loss of our culture. I promote cultural education tours for children because they need to know what other tribes are doing so they can develop a pride within themselves.

It takes one or two people to get others involved. I think that women should just get in there and try to help the community, whatever their needs are, especially the young people who represent our future generation. I don't think that we should just sit back and not do anything. I know through our own efforts that we can improve the living conditions of our communities.

Kaushee Harris

Kaushee (Emma) Harris, a Tlingit, was living in Atlin in 20
northern British Columbia. To support herself and her six chil-
dren she needed to upgrade her skills and get into the labour
market so she moved to Whitehorse, Yukon Territory, where
she now lives. She is the president of the Yukon Indian Women's
Association and is active in other groups.

Residential school was a long way from my home and I
used to have to stay there in the summer holidays because
it was too much trouble to send me so far for two months. I
was there until I was 12 then spent three years in a sanitorium with tuberculosis. When I did return home I was
scared my mother wouldn't like me or I wouldn't like her.

After separating from my alcoholic husband, I had to
support myself and my children. There were no jobs in
Atlin so I was on welfare for the first three years before I
decided to do something on my own. To me, being on welfare was a very humiliating experience. You have to account for the money and I was not able to give the children all the things they needed. Clothing had to be the
most inexpensive and only lasted a couple of washings.

When I came to Whitehorse and enrolled in school I was
afraid they would not accept me because I was out of
school for so many years by that time. With the education
I had I could take cooking, otherwise it would take years
before I could get into the work force. I couldn't wait
years, I had to do something immediately so I took cooking. I was very happy to have some means of supporting
my own family.

21   I've always been interested in the Indian movement but never had the opportunity to do anything because I've been raising my family and working. Then I got involved in the Yukon Indian Women's Association and got elected to go on a trip to a meeting of Indian Rights for Indian Women. Now we have started something we call the Fair Practices Committee to deal with discrimination. It's not just Indians but people who are interested. We hope to provide jobs for Indian people, especially the young ones. We haven't come up with any answers so far but we're still working on it. It takes a certain type of person to do this work, people who are not afraid to voice their opinions. Whitehorse is a small town and people think they will be remembered once they say something. It's like in the family, you want to keep the peace so you keep quiet.

I'm interested in doing things for Indian people – status, non-status, treaty or non-treaty. It's just too many people divided. We have too many things separating Indian people already. There are a lot of women interested and, although we are a very small group now, we'll grow. My main interest is to encourage children to get along within this fast moving society and to find new ways to make it easier for them to change a lot of things. The only way you can change something is to try and do it yourself.

Angie Todd-Dennis

Angie Todd-Dennis, 32, was born in the small northern British Columbia village of Fort St. James. Like most Carrier children she attended the Lejac Indian Residential school and then went on to finish high school in Dawson Creek, B.C. After obtaining her teaching certificate at the University of British Columbia, Angie taught for six years, three of these years in B.C. public schools in her home and on the Six Nations Reserve in Ontario. In 1973, Mrs. Dennis was chosen as a Canadian delegate to attend the World Peace Conference in Moscow. In the last two years she has worked on a home-school coordination program run by the Vancouver School Board. The work has involved liaison between home and school with native families. While at the University of British Columbia Angie developed an awareness of and interest in politics. She was asked to run in two provincial elections but declined. However, she took a plunge into Vancouver municipal politics when she ran for mayor at the age of 29. Although she lost, coming in fourth out of five candidates, she felt it served a purpose.

News reporters treated it as a big joke but the main reason I ran was to test this so-called democracy where an average person should be able to run. A lot of Indians have come up to me since and said how proud they were that I had tried.

She felt this gave many native people the motivation to run for office at various levels of provincial politics. When asked whether she plans to continue in the political arena, Angie replies that she would like to stay at home for a few years to raise her two sons, Robert, five and David, seven months. In discussing her life-long goals as a native person, Mrs. Todd-Dennis stressed the need for an education, not as the end-all but as a tool to change living conditions for her people. The loss of dignity of native people concerns her and she feels that material aid from the Department of Indian and Northern Affairs alone does not change attitudes.

It's difficult to change racist attitudes that are entrenched in society even at the tender age of six or seven. I've had students in grade two who were shocked to find out I was an Indian because I did not live in a teepee and eat snakes. I am anxious to see all school boards encourage the pre-history of Canada. After all, who was here to greet Columbus?

The issues that most concern Angie are a better education for native people, the breakdown of many native families, the high proportion of native children who are in custody and the number of Indians incarcerated in federal penitentiaries. The land claims are not a priority on her list since she feels that the problem won't be solved in her generation. However, because of its importance, she does support groups that are fighting the issue. Angie still grimaces when she discusses the paternalistic attitude of the government.

23   For years, I have battled bureaucratic red-tape in various ways. At 24, I sat in the membership office of the Department of Indian Affairs to try to regain my status which I had lost 14 years before when my mother married a non-Indian. I succeeded but fumed when they merely told me, "Sorry, we misinterpreted the Act." Another of my major accomplishments was to get involved in 1972, along with my husband, Clarence, in the now-famous Fred Quilt case. Clarence was then employed by the Union of B.C. Indian Chiefs. We travelled to the Stone Reserve in Northern British Columbia and got the statements of witnesses who alleged that Fred Quilt was kicked by an RCMP officer and died as a result of it. Although the Fred Quilt Committee succeeded, after a long media campaign, in forcing a second inquest into the death, no blame was attached to anyone. I still believe that Indian people have a long history of harassment by the RCMP because I myself have been harassed on occasions. I don't consider the results of the second inquest a failure because many eyes were opened and attitudes were changed. However, I am still cynical of the RCMP and I suppose most Indians are too. Why else have there been so few Indians going into the force? In my language, the name of the RCMP translates into "those who grab us".

Angie is now back attending the University of British Columbia part-time, taking courses in order to obtain her education degree.

Caroline Wesley

Caroline Wesley lives on the Queen Charlotte Islands and works with many women's groups. She helped found the Homemakers Club there and is vice-president of the B.C. Indian Homemakers Association. She is also treasurer for the National Committee, Indian Rights for Indian Women. She was married at 17 and has seven children, eight counting her granddaughter who has been with Caroline since she was born.

I've worked in a store and cooked in restaurants but other than that all my work has been volunteer. Someone came up here and spoke about Homemakers Clubs, then attended one of their conferences. Next year she couldn't make it so I was chosen to go and I've been going ever since. It's been eight years since I started with them. We raise money for children's parties, support recreation and help out in the home in any way we can. I think we've straightened out a lot of these band councils. They didn't want to have anything to do with women at all. They wouldn't listen but now they're starting to listen. I think women's groups would join together if they got the ones out who seem to be the pushers. They don't let the rest of the members know what's going on.

I'm what you call a liaison worker. There's a regional health and human resources council on the island and I attend meetings once a week and bring back information. We all get together here once a month, summarize these meetings and see how we're getting along. We've presented a brief to the B.C. government. If a person gets sick here, he has to go through so much bureaucracy just to get off the island, it's really crazy.

25   In Indian Rights for Indian Women we were involved in the Lavell case and cases of children being struck off the band list when their mothers married off the reserve. I think children should be the ones to decide whether they want status or not. I've started to attend the parent-teacher question-and-answer group. They're not getting enough physical education in the schools. A lot of small places don't have regular gym and there aren't enough recreation teachers. They're really hard to get. We'll have to train local people for a lot of these jobs.

Every year I go out to fish during May. That's why nobody bothers me during May. I have a smoke-house out back. Our family goes out across to Sandspit, stays there for a weekend and fishes. I used to stay a month and smoke and can the fish right there but now I bring it home. With the cost of living the way it is, I make sure I get my fishing done – then I know I have first-class food.

People are eventually going to move back here. They can't all live in the city. I think older people should be encouraging the young to marry Indians in order to retain our culture. One of the biggest problems is to get everyone involved in projects and work rather than just letting the most active people run things. I don't expect young people to be interested. You have to get them interested. If you get the main one going the rest will follow. I find there aren't enough hours in the day or days in the week.

Frances Woolsey

Frances Woolsey was born and raised in Whitehorse, Yukon. 26
She left school after completing grade ten but continued her education years later at the local vocational school after her husband died. Now she is director of the Yukon Indian Arts and Crafts Society.

My husband was a big-game outfitter and guide. When he died in a drowning accident in 1962, I was left with the hunting outfit and a large family to care for. I ran the business for three years then sold it as I found it too expensive to operate alone. It also took me away from home for six weeks every fall and my six children needed me. The work itself wasn't hard. I just couldn't make a profit as I had to hire people to do work I couldn't do, like driving the truck.

I took the commercial cooking course at the vocational school and a typing class at night. Then I got a job cooking at the Indian residential school in Whitehorse and I worked there for nine years – the last five years in a supervisory position. In 1970, I remarried, then in 1973 I helped set up a day-care centre for children aged from ten months to five years. It's run by a board of directors who come from all walks of life so we get involvement from everybody. I don't work there but I am the president of the board. It was hard getting the centre set up but since we opened our doors we have been filled to capacity – 40 children. It's not just Indian children. I don't believe in that. It's for everyone who needs day-care.

I left my job at the residential school in 1974 to work for the Yukon Indian Arts and Crafts Society promoting Indian handicrafts and reviving old traditions and skills

27 that are on the verge of being forgotten. We find outside markets and supply raw materials to the crafts people.

By selling their handicrafts and supplementing their incomes, people are helping themselves and taking pride in their work and their race. The main crafts are slippers, jackets, vests, etc. They are all heavily beaded on native tanned and smoked moose or caribou hide. I find this work very rewarding and satisfying as I deal with people every day.

I am a member of the local Indian Women's Association which joined other groups across Canada. It took awhile to get started but now Indian women are aware of what is going on and are making it their business to find out how to go about making life a bit better for their people in their own communities. I think this is good because it's the women who know what they need for children and families as they are responsbile for their well-being.

29

Vivian Ayoungman

Vivian Ayoungman comes from the Blackfoot reserve in southern Alberta. After graduating from the University of Calgary, she taught at reserve schools for three years then returned to the university as an academic counsellor for Indian students.

Education is important to me. It opened up new horizons, enlarged my view of life. My main interest now is getting Indian students into courses and helping to keep them in. I help them select their courses and work with them to solve some of their personal problems. Indian students going to university encounter various problems, such as those met by married students who increase their cultural awareness and become more conscious of injustices while at home, their wives stay left behind intellectually. One program I coordinated at Calgary was an orientation program for freshmen native students at the university. Another activity I helped organize was an academic night, a get-together to discuss academic problems.

Far too many Indian people assume that higher education means opting for dollars and losing their culture. It is not like that at all and the students at Calgary have shown that they care about their backgrounds. We formed a curriculum committee to assess the relevance to Indian people of some of the courses, then we made an outline for a course in Indian history. The history department at Calgary is interested in expanding in this area and has approved our course *History of the Indian of Western Canada.*

People responsible for the hiring of older Indians as resource people make the mistake of merely putting them in a classroom with young children. The elders want to tell

31   stories as they used to do but children are either too impatient to listen or perhaps do not understand. An alternative would be for the elders to teach the teachers, not the children. The elders have valuable knowledge to pass on and have a lot to contribute to education. They should be as adequately paid as other teachers.

   Besides those related to my job, I am involved in many other Indian activities. One of current interest is the formation of an Indian Scholars Association for all Indian graduates. I have done a lot of travelling all over Canada.

   In 1968 I was chosen as the national Indian Princess and one of the highlights was a trip to Holland with a Prairies inter-tribal dance group. My main function was in public relations so I was interviewed by radio and the press many times, appeared in parades and attended many Indian functions. Although I still enjoy attending rodeos and Indian Day celebrations, most of my time these days is spent in pursuing my career in education.

Caen Bly

Caen Bly has lived on the Blood reserve at Cardston since she   32
was born in 1944. Two of her passions are communications
and fitness through sports. She served as public relations officer
for the first Canadian Winter Games and on the board of direc-
tors for the 1975 games. Caen is editor of Kainai News.

I have always loved this reserve. It's dynamic, aggressive.
While I was at high school I helped on the ranch here,
driving a grain truck and looking after my own cattle.
When I married the manager of dad's ranch I sold out to
the reserve and became a housewife, just helping during
the summer months. Although I lost my status I didn't
want to move off. Dad warned us we might have to. Even
though I am not legally an Indian any more, I still identify
myself as one and personally, I would love to get my
status back.

    There was a communications gap between some of our
people here so with the help of a priest who was interested
in the community and its economic development, we for-
mulated the idea of Kainai News. It started out as a small
newsletter to spread information about new programs and
proposals the Bloods were thinking about. We literally
started from scratch with an untrained staff, small enough
to be flexible. We work together as a team. The newspaper is run on the principle that people who read it pay
for it. We don't want to make money but we want people
to help themselves. Kainai News got people so much involved in the community that there were 116 candidates
for one band council election. I think it has established a
lot of pride among people in Southern Alberta.

33　To be a good communications body you must be free from political and organizational parties. I believe in a free press. Newspapers and radio must be objective, but they can support the organizations by getting discussion started and getting ideas from people by letters to the editor. Our highest circulation is 3,500. In 1970, the Indian News Media Society was formed with Kainai News, *Blackfoot* and *Treaty No. 7* radio programs. Good concrete things have happened by making information available to people. Getting out helps me to see in perspective what's happening on my reserve. I'm not satisfied yet.

I feel that one of the most destructive things among Indian people is jealousy. Unfortunately a split still exists in communications in Alberta but with closer cooperation between native peoples this can be bridged. If I ever left the news media I would want to work in community development with people. I'm not an office person. My family has been very understanding, especially my husband, Ted. One of my biggest critics has been my dad, Fred Gladstone. He and my mum have been a great help to me both personally and in my job. My dad's interest is with people, not superficial things like money, fame or power.

Vicki Crowchild

Vicki Crowchild comes from a family of well-known Sarcee
chiefs. Her great-grandfather, Chief Bull Head, was present at
the signing of Treaty No. 7 in 1877 and her father, Chief Dave
Crowchild, had a bridge across the Bow River into Calgary, the
Crowchild Trail, named after him. Now her brother is a chief.
She believes the Calgary Stampede has helped Indian people
remember their skills and she would like to see people depend
more on themselves.

Indian people have participated in the Calgary Stampede
since 1912 and that has done an awful lot of good. It has
encouraged them to keep their culture. You know a lot of
Indians around here don't know how to make a teepee or
put it up. The older ones do but they don't pass it on. I
think there is still a need for it. At the Stampede the
women fix up the teepees and people live in them. I'd like
to see that continue.

I was brought up on the Sarcee reserve near Calgary.
There are about 600 people living there now. At one time
I got the job as band secretary. Now I work for the Department of Indian and Northern Affairs in social work. I'd
like to see more effort directed towards the prevention of
problems rather than just giving welfare. Government
gives you something, then takes it away, like the students'
personal allowance. To me this was good because it gave
incentive to children to go to school. If they didn't go they
were docked for that day. It was the first time the younger
generation had to work for something.

On some reserves, Indian people are reluctant to take
on their own responsibilities. When the government

35   stops helping, the people think it has given up its responsibility. Some reserves are afraid because they think the direct line to Ottawa is no longer there. They should depend more on themselves. It is time to change but it's not going to happen overnight. It may take years.

My concern about native women is that they should become a united body and respect the views and ideas of each side so that maybe there could be an answer to this status question or any issue. If you walk down the street, people can't recognize you as status or non-status, they just see that you are native so the piece of paper saying you're status doesn't make any difference. You know you're Indian. You can get on a bandwagon on one issue and forget about everything else that is important – like neglect of children and alcoholism.

One minute you're feeding alcoholics, teaching them to drink, and the next minute you're trying to cure them. What's the answer? I think part of the funding for activities should go to trying to prevent, rather than starting the other way around saying, "Here's the liquor. Go to it. We're going to teach you how to drink", which is one of the things I heard. Some of the woman-power should go to these issues. Some reserves are starting detoxification centres which is good.

I have to live in the city because of the necessity but on some occasions I wish I was back on the reserve for peace and quiet and to get away from noise pollution.

Marie Marule

Marie Marule is a Blood who grew up on the reserve at Cardston. 36
While at university, she became interested in Indian organiza-
tions and after spending four years with CUSO in Africa she
returned to Canada to work with her own people. For the last
few years she has assisted George Manuel, president of the
National Indian Brotherhood.

University was terrifying at first. You are made to feel that
you are just not as smart as non-Indians and that going to
university is a little beyond your capacity. I was really
afraid I would fail. It was more psychological than anything else.

Then I found out how naive I was about the white community and how patronizing people were to us. Canadians
just don't see themselves as colonials. I developed a real
anger and frustration and was made into a racist. Then I
realized that being a racist, I was no better. Racism is no
answer.

I went to work in Zambia and loved it there. I didn't
want to come back but when I was growing up, there was
never any question in my mind that whatever I learned I
must use on behalf of my own people. It was no conscious
decision. It was just there, a fact. So I came back and since
have worked with George Manuel. It has been fascinating.

I see things in a broader perspective than I used to and
regret that more people haven't had that exposure. We
tend to feel that our problems are isolated, but they are
not. I felt a gap growing between myself and my own community. My reaction to people has changed and sometimes
it is difficult for my own people to understand me, what I

37 say and how I act, but I have had to learn to play all the psychological games white people play, like putting people down. That becomes part of you and changes you.

Once you are politically aware of certain things in the decision-making process you can't withdraw yourself. I get mad because so many Canadians say "that is political." Everything is political. When people refuse to make a decision they actually make one. They don't realize that by not making it they have put that decision on somebody else.

What I am really concerned about is development of respect for groups with different cultural backgrounds. Insofar as I don't want anyone to destroy mine, I don't want to destroy anyone else's either.

I am convinced that our total situation is worse now than it was 50 years ago, mentally, socially, culturally. It used to be possible to recognize Indians even if they did not look like Indians, because of the way they would look into your eyes. We were open with each other. That has changed. Now there is much more guardedness, a caution we did not have before. Until we can deal with each other – whites and Indians – as one human being with another, with rights to govern and direct our own courses, it is just going to be a continued deterioration.

Flora Zaharia

Flora Zaharia is a Blood woman with a tremendous amount of energy. Born on the Blood reserve in Alberta, she now lives in Winnipeg and uses her innovative ideas for helping children as a guidance counsellor in an inner city school. She has been teaching school most of her adult life.

School has to be interesting, has to be fun. But if home isn't fun and children can't get enough sleep, then it is hard for school to be fun. I worry about what is going to happen to the kids here in this school. Many come from poor homes and have a very hard life. About one-third of them are Indian or Metis.

When I left school I was going to be a nurse, then I went to Montreal to study to be a nun but I found it lonely and austere. That's where I learned French. I speak Blackfoot too so I'm tri-lingual. Later I went to the University of Calgary and got my first year of teacher training, then went to teach at a residential school and attended summer school.

In 1959, I came to Winnipeg for a holiday and worked with Office Overload for a change but soon I wanted to get back to a classroom. For two years I was principal on the Norway House reserve, then I got married and, except for time off to have my two children, have been teaching and counselling ever since.

Six years ago I started working towards getting native liaison workers for inner-city schools to help children caught in the city with difficult home lives. It took five years before the Winnipeg school division accepted but now we have several workers and I am trying to get more

39 and get better pay for them. I have been on boards of directors for organizations such as the Friendship Centre, Children's Aid Society, Little Ones School, International Centre, Manitoba Metis Federation, Manitoba Social Steering Committe.

I am also one of the team members of Tawow Project Canada West and the native social studies committee. The object of Project Canada West is to give Indian and Metis people a better knowledge of their background so they can accept who they are; and to give non-Indians an opportunity to appreciate Indian culture. We looked through text books being used in social study classes and found the usual stereotypes of Indians as savages killing priests and pictures of them torturing people. We need some good Indian historians and writers to put out new books. We put together a multi-media kit which includes study cards, a teacher's resource book, tapes, film strips, handicrafts and games such as quizzes and crossword puzzles.

I love my work and my family and have a very happy marriage. My husband and I go out together once a month and do a lot of sports together. He doesn't mind me gadding around on all these committees. I wouldn't have been what I am now if I had not had a really good man behind me. He is very understanding.

Crees

41

Eleanor Brass

At 70, Eleanor Brass is a very humorous and lively lady with plenty of confidence. She was not always so outgoing. Born on the Peepeekeesis reserve in Saskatchewan, she was shy and quiet whenever she left the reserve but her late husband encouraged her to stand up for herself and to be a writer. She is a descendant of two chiefs, one Cree and one Saulteaux, who signed Treaty No. 4 in 1874. Now she is living at Peace River, Alberta.

I quit school before I finished grade 12 because I was crazy about my boyfriend. We got married when I was 19 and were very happy together. My husband was self-educated but he had a lawyer's mind and taught me a lot. When he

died in 1965 we had been married 40 years. I wanted to die too because part of me had gone with him. Our life had not been easy and we worked very hard.

When we first went to live in Regina not many Indian people were living off the reserves. For a time we lived on File Hills reserve but I háted it, there was no recreation and I missed all the interesting things I had found to do outside. I remember I used to get in fights with the Indian agent on the reserve who was very dictatorial. That was back in the twenties when women did not speak up for themselves.

During the thirties we got a job on a dairy farm. That was the first time I went on a train and I was very thrilled. We had a nice little cottage with running water but the work was too hard. I had to get up at 3:30 a.m. to milk the cows by hand. My hands swole up like boxing gloves. I kept falling asleep while I was milking, dreaming I was sitting amongst painted teepees, but it was spotted cows. After that we went to Nipawin to work on a cousin's farm and I looked after an old couple. I was paid five dollars a month. In winter, we went back to the reserve and we told the other Indians what went on outside and got them to form social clubs. When we went to live in Regina again I did all kinds of jobs, including scrubbing floors.

I used to talk to my husband about how we managed to live in the city and what it was like for Indians to live off the reserve. He told me to write it all down, exactly as it happened to us, so I did and sent it to the Regina newspaper, The Leader-Post. They published it and asked me to write more. Then I began to realize that our Indian

43 stories were going to be lost if they weren't written down so I wrote a lot of articles and stories.

When I was over 40 I went to business school, took lessons in public speaking and I worked for the Saskatchewan Arts Board lecturing on Indian art. At festivals I showed a display of Indian artifacts. For years I was with the YWCA, first as a cook, then teaching. I had a puppet class and a handicraft class. I belonged to the United Nations Association and helped in starting the Regina Friendship Centre. We never had any children of our own so our home became a kind of friendship centre for kids.

There was only $100 in the bank when my husband died so I went on working. I was an information officer with the Department of Agriculture and worked on a radio program. It was a talk show about various things in agriculture. I think my most interesting program was about rats: there is a myth that there are no rats in Saskatchewan. I was a placement officer and counsellor too and had to work with chiefs on the reserves and Metis people.

After I retired I came to Peace River to work for the Friendship Centre, then to the Alberta Native Communications Society. Three-quarters of the people up here are native and I want to collect some of the history of this area. I am doing public relations for the chapter of the Voice of Alberta Native Women's Society.

Do you know the story about the Indians on the moon? When the Americans first landed on the moon they saw two Indians sitting on a log. The Americans hailed them through a loudspeaker and the Indians said to each other, "Oh, no. Not again."

Amy Clemons

The Amy Clemons Tiny Tots Nursery School in Selkirk, Manitoba is named for a Cree woman who was born on the St. Peter's reserve in 1906. After working in the Winnipeg Friendship Centre for six years, Amy knew the problems of families coming to town from their reserves, so she started a centre for them in Selkirk where she lives. This led to the formation of the nursery school. In 1970, Manitoba named her Woman-of-the-Year and in 1973 she was awarded the Order of Canada.

We were concerned about the people that come from up north, out of the reserves, moving into town to take different kinds of courses. They bring their families with them and they're kind of lost. Some of them were missing their homes. That's what made us visit them and help them get acquainted, to get to know the town and the routine of town life. I took the school principal's wife around to native homes and introduced her and got the names of children. We found out that there were a lot of children who needed pre-schooling, a lot of backward children who were shy and talked in their own language.

Being brought up with non-Indian people is really difficult. One of the native children wasn't used to speaking English. They couldn't do anything with him and they got me to talk to him in my language and in three days time he was a different child. He just took that long to get socialized and mix with other children. That was a wonderful thing.

At first, there was a teacher for the pre-schoolers and she just had four or five children around her listening to stories. That's how it got started and it grew and grew and we started getting volunteers to help. You need a lot of help in a nursery school and we encouraged the mothers to come and help. That's good too for these women. We rented a hall, then a church basement and now we're building our own school. We have about 70 children from age two and when they get to be four or five they are ready for kindergarten. The children get used to other children, play games together, then they're not backward or shy any more. They stay half a day and another group comes the other half. There's no room for them all to come at the same time. They keep taking children. They don't turn anyone away and they've got their hands full.

I had wonderful parents, a very strict father who knew education was what we needed. I liked school but my mother would take my brothers and I to work in gardens, earning a dollar a day, to make enough money to get winter clothes. We'd work until snow fell in late October or first part of November so I would miss a lot of school, yet I was the highest. If I'd had an opportunity like some children today . . .

I've always worked in institutions. When I was a girl I started in a hospital and there were lots of times they asked

me to interpret and I always tried. I always kept up my own language and was able to be understood by people who spoke Saulteaux. Cree and Saulteaux aren't much different to me. Most of the young people then were ashamed of their identity, ashamed to speak their language and they lost it because they wouldn't try. If you don't speak it every day you forget. I still visit hospitals; I like making people happy. A lot of them are lonely and like their own kind of people to visit them so they can speak their own tongue. There's a lot of good work from non-native people going round visiting, but it's not the same thing.

I sensed a lot of discrimination in Winnipeg, like finding rooms for people to live in. I'd see an ad in the paper and phone and they'd say, "Oh yes, come right over," but as soon as they saw I was Indian they'd say, "Oh sorry, it's taken," and "Oh, I forgot to take the sign down." They'd make a lot of petty excuses.

People make such mistakes when they don't judge Indians individually but as a group. When they see chronic alcoholics day after day they think that's what all Indians are like. But there are a lot of good, intelligent Indians right across Canada. They forget to mention those. There are still some native women who are poor volunteers and they need to come out and get in with the activities, join in different things. That's the way you learn. A lot of them think they don't know what to do. They're afraid to challenge anything for fear they do wrong. They're shy. That's why they don't talk right away. They want to make sure they're right first of all, then they get pushed aside.

Irene Desjarlais

Irene Desjarlais, from the Cowessess reserve in Saskatchewan, is one of a family of eight children and now has eight of her own. During the war she trained as a nurse at the Brandon General Hospital and now is in charge of the Health and Welfare Canada Indian Health Centre in Fort Qu'Appelle, Saskatchewan. Irene loves her work and sees the need for more native nurses.

I always wanted to be a nurse, like an older Indian girl I knew who was my idol, and my mother encouraged me. Also, one of my teachers bought me a watch, a pen and bandage scissors to go in training. My first day at Brandon General I was so scared I felt like turning around and running away down the steps and home. This was the first time away from my people. I heard someone say that I'd be just like the rest of the Indians and quit, wasting the government's money, so I decided I'd show him that Indians are not quitters. I was determined. I graduated in 1945 and passed my RN exams that fall. Several years later, my younger sister, Connie, also became a registered nurse.

Life was hard when I was a child during the depression. My mother was widowed and kept the farm going and we children had to pick wild berries and work in the garden to put food away for the winter. She received five dollars a month as mother's allowance. I grew up in a residential school where you were punished if you spoke your native language and, though both my parents spoke Cree and Saulteaux, they didn't teach it to us because of this situation in school. Missionaries in those days taught the children that the Indian way of life was wrong so we weren't allowed to be Indian for ten months of every year. What a glorious two month holiday we had at home on the reserve each summer. We always taught my children that they were Indian and they have never been ashamed of it, which makes us feel good.

While I was working at Brandon hospital, I came to Fort Qu'Appelle to visit and the matron of the Indian Hospital

47 persuaded me to work for them. I resigned at Brandon and
    have worked in Fort Qu'Appelle for 21 years. In 1967, I
    came into public health and two years later went back to
    university to get my diploma. It was really difficult; I had
    been out of school for 24 years and had to leave home and
    live by myself for a year. I'd never have been able to do
    this without the help of my husband and children. By then
    my children were mostly grown up. In the clinic here, we
    see children and adults, both sick and well, mostly well.
    We advise them if they need to see a doctor rather than
    treat them here as is done in the north. Although most
    older people see the need for health care, the younger
    generation is improving; in fact, many are really with it.
    We immunize the children and urge women to breastfeed
    their babies.

    When I go on the reserves I know many of the people
    from seeing them in the hospital during the years I worked
    there. Having lived on the reserve, one can understand
    the people and empathize with them. The days I go to do
    home visits, I come back and feel so great. You know, some
    people even thank you for coming. The nurses I work with
    are wonderful but there's a real need for more native
    nurses also.

    Things are improving for the Indian people. With the
    wisdom and guidance of the elders, along with education,
    both academic and in native culture, the younger genera-
    tion should proudly take their place in society and once
    more hold their head high as did our proud and noble
    ancestors.

Jean Folster

In 1971, Jean Folster, a Swampy Cree from Norway House, 48
became the first Indian woman to be appointed magistrate. She
had already been chief of the biggest band in Manitoba for
three years. She has lived all her life in Norway House, a settle-
ment of 2,400 people at the north end of Lake Winnipeg. In
1973, she received the second annual award of the Canadian
Speech Association for her contribution to communication and
understanding between people. (Former Prime Minister John
Diefenbaker had been given the first award.) Jean speaks Cree
and English.

Grade eight is as far as our school on the reserve goes and
that's all the schooling I had. Now we have about 300
children there and they have to go off the reserve for high
school. But we're building a new school which will go up
to grade 12 if the children want to stay home. When I was
16, I went to work at the hospital as a laundress and after
six years, I got married and had eight children. My husband was drowned in a storm in 1953 so I've been on my
own a long time.

Norway House was one of the first reserves to take over
responsibility for the administration of welfare from the
Department of Indian and Northern Affairs. I worked as a
welfare administrator counselling families and for a year I
was a band council member assigned to health and welfare.
Then I was asked to run for chief because I knew a lot
about problems. We had a council of two women, four
men and me as chief. I was 45 years old when I had my
first trip off the reserve; that was in 1968 when I went to
Winnipeg to a welfare administration conference.

49   When I was first appointed magistrate by the provincial government, I was scared as I didn't know my duties. I preside over the family court and deal with minor cases of drunkenness. I only deal with the guilty pleas and remand all the "not guilty" pleas to other magistrates. The court sits once a month in all of the five main communities and I go to all the isolated places when people can't come to me. Our number one problem is drinking, abuse of alcohol, even though we don't have a liquor store on the reserve, only a beer outlet at the hotel. One time it ran out of beer. That was the first quiet Sunday we ever had.

Mostly, the RCMP service is good on the reserve but they have to follow rules and do what they are told. People want the policemen to be able to act on their own here. As it is now, people often just won't lay charges. There needs to be more understanding of the law by Indian people and more communication at the community level. Hardly anyone attends meetings so I think we need a local radio station. I don't know what is going to happen to the lives of people affected by the dams being built on the Churchill and Nelson Rivers and the flooding of the community of South Indian Lake. Manitoba Hydro said it will compensate people but we don't really believe that.

We are living in a changing world today. It is a time where there's a growing concern for everyone's rights and privileges. We often hear only the news that makes headlines or is very dramatic and it often builds up and supports the prejudices that we all have. I think Indian people can help to show an example to all Canadians if we make an effort to work together and communicate as a people.

Verna Kirkness

Verna Kirkness was born on the Fisher River reserve in Manitoba. Education is her main interest as she sees it as a preparation for living and a means of providing a free choice of where to live and work. While she was Director of Education for the Manitoba Indian Brotherhood, Verna co-edited Indians Without Tipis, a book that explains some feelings and hopes of Indian and Metis people. This book forms part of a kit sponsored by Project Canada West to improve classroom material in Canadian schools. Verna is presently Education Director with the National Indian Brotherhood in Ottawa.

It was in high school that I first questioned what it was to be an Indian. There were no other native students and I had a feeling of inferiority. The other people there did not give me that feeling. They were good. It was within myself. This personal experience led me to an awareness of the importance of growing up with a positive self-image. Schools and the media tend to destroy this concept in us by their expression of negative aspects of Indian people. I am very concerned about the exaggerations and injustices done to the Indian people in history books written by white people. All too often the Indian is seen as the bad guy. He steals, cheats, kills mercilessly; he's dirty and drunken; he's a loser. I worry about what these pictures do to the white youngsters who have no personal contact with Indians and what they do to Indian self-esteem. Indian youngsters are being taught as if they were from urban, middle-class white society. There is little relevance in the learning process for the Indian child.

Though 40 per cent of Indian children in Manitoba enter school with little or no facility with English, recognition of Indian languages within the school system has been very recent. For many years children were punished for using their own language and therefore left with the impression that Indian languages are inferior. A positive and practical approach to the problem is to give instruction in the child's own tongue for the first few years. During this time English can be taught as a second language. Traditionally, Indian education took a practical form. Children were taught by their parents and grandparents but few parents nowadays view the school in the community as

51 *their* school. The present trend is for Indian people to control their own educational system, to determine the curriculum and to employ teachers with skills relevant to the Indian way of life. In this way, the school would belong to the community, not to the teachers.

Learning is not a privilege for only the young to enjoy; it is a life-time process. There are opportunities for drop-outs to start anew but often Indian people in remote areas do not know these opportunities exist. I feel many who enroll in up-grading programs do not complete their courses because of the inadequate counselling that precedes enrollment.

Indian education has been governed by civil servants for over 100 years. When the federal government adopted a policy in 1973 enabling Indian bands to control their own education, it was an historic breakthrough. The process of implementation of "Indian control of Indian education" is beset with problems because to realize such policy is to eventually do away with the hierarchy of civil servants that for years had authority to govern Indians.

We are in pursuit of honour and justice. Institutions and the media must promote Indians and "Indianness" in a positive manner. We firmly believe that if we know and understand ourselves and if others know and understand us, progress will be made that will affect the total Canadian society.

Mary Ann Lavallee

Mary Ann Lavallee, a Saulteaux-Cree, has always lived on the Cowessess reserve where her husband, Sam, farmed for 35 years. Life on the reserve and circumstances surrounding these many years of farming gave her the impetus and the courage to speak her mind. This became a starting point for her life-long commitment to her search for social justice for Indian people.

Her struggle for the pursuit of life, liberty and happiness for herself and her family demanded that she become involved in the fight for a better quality of life for all reserve residents. It meant that she had to dive into the politics of everyday life on the reserve which included the struggle for better housing, better educational opportunity and economic and social reform.

Mary Ann says, "Because of their tribal systems, the individual initiative, identity of the Indian, and the free enterprise system has been non-existent. In addition, the Indian Act was instituted as law to enforce the Treaties, to administer the lives of Indians, to protect them from outright annihilation, and to keep them out of the way of encroaching European settlement of their lands. This is why so many Indian people today do not know how to live as responsible individuals. The result is too much dependence on government, social welfare, and alcohol. However, Indian people at large are now beginning to realize that they have rights as individuals and as human beings and that they also have rights and responsibilities as a group distinct from all other Canadians."

To add to her beliefs and convictions, Mary Ann has been actively involved for the past 26 years. From 1950-1967, she was an instigator and active supporter of the new Home and School Association on her reserve, and she became very active in supporting women's activities long before the government grants of today were available.

She is a firm believer in equal educational opportunities and freedom of choice for Indian parents in decisions that affect their children. She was instrumental in the formation of province-wide school committees on reserves in Saskatchewan as well as kindergarten programs for Indian children – both of which were established by the Department of Indian and Northern Affairs in the mid-sixties.

Her active interest in economic reform began in 1960 because of the ever present spectre of bankruptcy hanging on the horizon of the Lavallee farm. All else having failed, Sam and Mary Ann plunged into the political arena in an attempt to keep the farm and home alive. Because Section 89 of the Indian Act makes it impossible for any Indian on the reserve to produce land title to use as collateral for a farm loan, the struggle to gain access to the financial vaults of Canada involved a span of approximately ten years. This struggle lasted through three successive federal governments involving several Ministers of Indian and Northern Affairs and several members of Parliament. The federal Minister of Agriculture, the Honourable Alvin Hamilton, P.C., M.P., brought this issue into parliamentary debate after a personal visit to Sam's farm. Finally in 1969, after years of patient correspondence with the Department of Indian and Northern Affairs and various government departments, Mary Ann went to Ottawa to receive the personal signature of the Honourable Jean Chretien, Minister of Indian Affairs and Northern Development, on documents that would henceforth be used as collateral in lieu of land title. Thus, for the first time in

53 *the history of Canada, the doors to high finance were officially and quietly opened to Indians. Simultaneously, Sam's farm was saved and his farming career assured.* Mary Ann says, "Because of this new legislation, the Indian Act received a resounding wallop."

Because of deep personal convictions and voluntary personal involvement over the years she became a public speaker in her own right. For 12 years, she travelled across Canada as an unofficial spokeswoman of Indian people seeking out social justice and social reform.

Mary Ann says that, "To work for a better quality of life for your own people is loving and serving your country. Never before in the long history of the Indian nation has the challenge of survival been more acute and pertinent. Of necessity, we Indian people will have to reassess our present situation to see how it stacks up against the forces of modern technology. We will have to dig deeper than the obvious to pull out the roots of our discontent. We will have to focus special attention on our identity as individuals and as a nation so that eventually we will not need the federal government to identify us as numbers or, to tell us who we are. The task of identity is our own. It was handed down to us over a thousand or so years ago by our ancestors who roamed this great land.

"The Indian people are Canada's first peoples, truly Canada's founding nation. In order to survive as such, Indian people will have to chart a new course that will demand of all true Indians a new unswerving loyalty plus a new identification and acceptance of ever increasing responsibilities that are geared to future progress and survival in the years to come. Above all, it is imperative that we Indians once again recognize our God – in whatever name He comes to us: the Saviour, Great Spirit or Kitche-Manitou. Thus shall we triumph over the destructive forces of today.

"It is a foregone conclusion that a tremendous amount of dedicated work and commitment faces the Indian woman of today. The task of rekindling the Indian culture, rebuilding the Indian nation, is placed in her arms. The Indian nation rests it weary head upon her bosom. She is its mother and she must give it life, love and nourishment so that it will grow healthy, strong and magnificent. I have great faith in Indian women," says Mary Ann, who refers to Indian women as Canada's last frontier.

Margaret White

Margaret White was born at Hobbema, Alberta and completed 54
grade four on the reserve. For over 15 years she has been working
on skid row in Vancouver and in 1974 was given the Good
Citizen award. She was the first native woman to receive it.

For a time I worked as a nurse's aide in hospitals but
didn't like the way they were treating the patients, so I
quit. When people from home knew I had moved to Vancouver, they said, "Would you please, if you have time,
look for our girl. We know she's there somewhere." My
goodness, I didn't find one, I found many – in horrible
conditions too. The next thing was to find a house, a
home. I knew what to do and how to help. Then we had
to form an organization. If you want to collect money you
have to register under a societies act and have a board and
on and on. The board was all white people and the
minute they got their feet in they became "experts" and
started putting down policies. One woman said I was
discriminating because I was only taking Indian girls. We
got the place going because the public wanted a place for
Indian girls but the board had other ideas. It's when you
get this damned little board in there . . . when someone can
do a job they should be allowed to do it without having
their hands tied. Then they started bringing in old women
and mental patients. Well, I didn't take the job to work
with mental patients so I quit, then started another group.
After five months the new place was running well, then
"they" started getting big ideas on how it should be run.
That collapsed too and I said, "That's it, I'm not doing
any more."

55 I'd lived on skid row for practically two years, lived down there and knew the girls. So many of them have died and it's so sad. These young people weren't bad, they'd just had a hard time. They had to do anything to survive, to eat, to live. They weren't bad. They were so good to me, just unbelievable – then to see them die. Oh God!

One girl called me to come and see her, please. So I went down and she really was sick, burning with fever. We had to walk a ways to the car. I was almost carrying her, her suitcase, my purse, her purse. Do you think anyone would help me? They just stood and looked at us. She wouldn't go in the ambulance, she wanted to go in my car. The girls called it "our" car. She died that week.

When I quit the second house, a friend of mine said, "You can't let those girls down," so we got another house going and this one still exists. I had to go and speak to groups. Church groups, women's groups, they realized the problem. We had good support in one sense.

Now things have changed so badly. The girls are heavy into drugs. Sometimes someone will phone me during the night as high as anything and not knowing what they're talking about but they're desperate and I just listen. I look back on much of it as a bad experience having to see people live that way and go hungry in a rich land like this. I haven't really done that much to change things.

Jane Willis

Jane Willis, a Swampy Cree from Fort George on James Bay, had her first glimpse "outside" when she went to high school in Sault Ste. Marie, Ontario. Unable to get a job back home she went to live in California and, while raising her four children, she wrote about her own childhood. The book Geniesh *brought her many job opportunities and she came back to Canada. To interview some of the women whose stories are included in this book, Jane visited reserves for the first time. She was surprised to find women of other tribes were like her own people in James Bay.*

When I left Fort George to go to school, I had mixed feelings. Nobody had ever gone to high school before. While I was curious about seeing the rest of the world, I didn't really want to leave home. It was a painful choice. I had been brought up to believe that white people were smarter and not even my above-average grades could convince me otherwise. For 18 years I tried to get jobs in Fort George but people kept telling me I wasn't qualified, then I'd see white people with fewer qualifications getting the jobs. I had been told to make something of myself, to show that not all Indians were savages or stupid, and yet I was given no chances to prove otherwise. What pride and self-confidence I'd had were quickly destroyed.

My book started out as an article I sent to a magazine and had rejected. A friend thought it was very interesting and suggested I write a book. I thought it was a great joke, "Me, write a book." I did a few chapters anyway and he became so interested that he insisted on doing it himself.

When I hesitated, he told me I couldn't do it. That was all I needed to get going. I had to prove him wrong. That's how the whole thing started. To me, finishing the book was the big achievement. I never expected it to sell and I didn't think it would affect my life at all. I was very naive. After my book was published, the same people who had been turning me down were suddenly offering me jobs. I became a little bitter and turned them down saying, "I'm no more qualified now than I was before."

When the book first came out, the kids in Fort George used to stare at me and I'd feel like a museum piece or something, but to the older people, my mother especially, it was just another of my crazy stunts. There, I know people aren't judging me because of the book. I'm me. My children enjoy it up there. They prefer it to a city. They're used to all that freedom. They can go wherever they want and not worry about trespassing on somebody's property. It's an island so they can't get lost. Everybody knows who they are. I have a shack there, a sort of retreat, some place to go back to.

With the James Bay project, everything changed overnight. It was a very independent society. The people were self-sufficient and never had welfare or housing programs like the reservations. They had to fend for themselves and they were very happy. But then another way of life was thrown at them suddenly and the old people, particularly, didn't have time to get used to it gradually. It was a big shock to them. They don't like what's going on but they learn to accept everything. The old people are strong. I can't speak for the younger people. I know there's a lot of

57 confusion in their lives but I think they also prefer the old ways. People up there are still very happy.

When I was growing up, things like modern conveniences seemed very important. I thought I could never go back to Fort George and do without them again but I have. After a while, you look back and wonder why. If you use your head at all, you know that's not what is important in life – it's people.

In James Bay people haven't been exposed to white society that long and they are very natural and unaffected. You don't have to worry about playing games. You can be yourself and not have to worry about trying to give a good impression. Standards are different up there. Success, money and titles don't mean much. When I was growing up we believed everything we saw in the movies. To us, the whole world was filled with cowboys and Indians . . . and we always cheered for the cowboys. All I'd been taught about other Indians was that they were a wild bunch of alcoholics and prostitutes and I guess I believed it because I was afraid of mixing with other Indians and of going on reserves.

I could go to any Indian community in James Bay and feel perfectly at home but it was different down south. Then I was asked to do some interviewing for this book and it really opened my eyes. I went to a few reserves and was surprised that they weren't that much different from Fort George. Some of them were very depressing, of course, and seemed to have lost all hope, but all the women I met were just like people at home – not spoiled, just down to earth and honest.

Metis

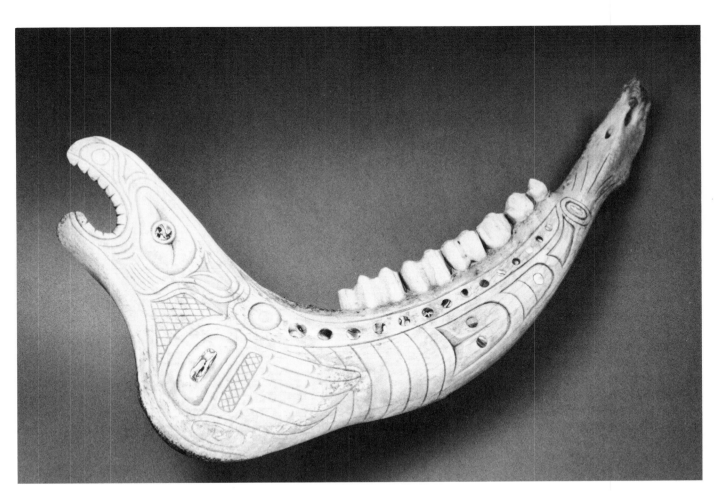

Maria Campbell

Maria Campbell is a half-breed of Cree, Scots and French descent. She was born and raised on a trap line in Saskatchewan, north-west of Prince Albert. She has told her story in the book Half-Breed. *In her book, Maria vividly projects a half-breed's social and political oppression, and at the same time captures the half-breed's joys and contributions. Her childhood was filled with poverty and poetry, literature and love. Over all this was the ever-present understanding of a great-grandmother she called Cheechum. This old woman's spirit sustained Maria throughout her troubled life. Protected by her great grandmother's love and wisdom, Maria did not know shame and degradation until her formal education began, first in a residential school, then in a country school surrounded by white children. Maria remembers that as being the beginning of a nightmare that, for her, lasted 20 years.*

Starting school was the beginning of my fear. I was not allowed to speak Cree and I spoke very poor English. The teachers tried to make me a model white student. At home I could not speak English because my parents and grandmother were very traditional. They did not understand the white man's ways and, if they did, they could do nothing to help me. The only time I could ever be myself was on the piece of land that separated me from school and family.

Tragic accidents led Maria at 15 into a marriage in a hopeless attempt to keep her seven motherless brothers and sisters together. When the marriage failed, the welfare authorities stepped in and the children were taken from her. Maria fled to Van-

couver where drugs, alcohol and prostitution became a means of survival and a way of life.

I had to learn the hard way. When I finally recovered from the years I had spent hooked on drugs I realized that, like many of my people, I was full of fears. Fear to be what I wanted to be. For years I had been told how to live and think. I had only known teachers, missionaries, policemen and welfare workers. I remember my Cheechum telling me about people wearing blankets to protect themselves. I never understood what she meant until now. She used to say, "the blanket does not provide warmth, it only destroys them. To come out from under it means to face reality, ugly as it is, but to be able to do that is to be free." It was hard to throw that blanket away but I realized that the realities under it were just as ugly as those outside.

Maria threw her blanket away and gradually rebuilt her life. She worked at everything from hairdresser to housemaid. She tried to help other girls on skid row who were facing the same problems she had.

I realized I could not solve their personal problems but I knew how important it was to just have someone to talk to and a place to go for food and shelter. However, the more involved I became with street work, the angrier I became. Society is much harsher on women than it is on men. Native women have always been portrayed as unfeeling, wild and dirty by historians and later by movies

61 and television. This, coupled with the traditions of white society which regard women as inferior, made the realities for a native woman on the street pretty hopeless. Perhaps the attitude of native men towards their women was the most painful because, along with the white man's stereotypes, there is the ancient Indian belief that women have special powers. The missionaries who came exploited this sacred belief by impressing on us that women were a source of evil. The oppression of native people will never end until these myths are recognized and destroyed.

Maria's work on the street led to the opening of the first halfway house in Alberta for women. She became active in the Native Rights Movement in the early sixties. However, she dropped out of active work in the Metis Association in 1970 when she saw that the huge grants from government were not the answer for her people.

I remember Cheechum warning me about handouts from the government saying, "When the government gives you something, it takes all that you have in return – your pride, your dignity, everything that makes you a living soul." I saw our people being divided and fighting with each other over government money and I understood what she meant. I did not want to be a part of that.

Maria has written two more books, The Indians of the Plains *and the first of a series of children's books,* Little Badger and the Fire Spirit. *She has written a screen play for the National Film Board titled* The Red Dress *and numerous radio and television scripts. She's also half-way through a novel and is working on a screen play for half-breeds. She will be starting a syndicated radio program of her own this fall on women's rights. Maria is the mother of four children and has one grandson. She is the wife of Shannon Two-Feathers, singer-composer and artist.*

Bertha Clark

Bertha Clark, president of the Voice of Alberta Native Women's Society for several years, and first president of the Native Women's Association of Canada formed in 1974, finds plenty of leadership among native women if it can be brought out. Of Cree descent, Bertha was born in the Peace River country of Alberta and now lives in Fort McMurray. Her own leadership qualities come from her father, "a great organizer in his community," and from her Air Force training as a sports instructor.

Dad insisted on helping our neighbours, even the white homesteaders coming into the community. He showed them how to build their cabins and there was always trading back and forth. Everyone attended the same school and I can remember we all went to social functions like the community dance. Nobody stayed home, even the smallest baby. I was always very shy and in the background and really wasn't sure what I wanted to do, then I went into the Air Force and was asked whether I'd like to take an instructor's course because I was interested in sports. It was a frightening experience to be out on the parade ground but we organized all the recreation for the base for men and women.

I started working with native groups when I got involved with Nistawayou. That's a Cree word meaning the joining of three rivers, a place where people would meet. It was a voluntary organization with housing committees. Now it has gone into Friendship Centres. Then I was involved in Newstart, a government research program for upgrading native people, and after that I was hired as a family counsellor. We were given a short crash course but counselling comes from practical experience. When I worked directly with native families it showed me that they really had a lot of difficulties in isolated areas and didn't know how to cope with city life.

The Voice of Alberta Native Women's Society has done a lot for native women: treaty, non-status and Metis. We look upon ourselves as native mothers making a better way of life for all native women, especially those in re-

63 mote parts of the province. There are about 600 members and 23 chapters. We concentrate on getting people on reserves and in isolated communities organized, find out what they would like to do and work with them. Unless people want them, there is not much use developing programs. Not everybody wants the same thing and we don't feel we should go in and say this is what they should do. We want to hear it from them. We have 12 activity centres and bring women from isolated communities for two or three-day workshops. When they go back, if they want to form an organization, one of our directors goes in and helps them set it up. Then the women have to tell us what they want to do: homemaking, personal development, basic life skills, make drapes, do upholstery or just anything they want to do and hopefully we will find funding to get them working out of their centre.

As native mothers we'd like to work with families before they get bored, before the damage is done. We want to work with families on prevention programs for alcohol and drugs. We want to get parents working and playing with their children. We did a lot of recreation with Newstart and people really enjoyed it.

It's a big job but a worthwhile step. Working with people is like being a housewife in that your work is never done because there are always new people cropping up and wanting to get interested and involved. They respond very well but they do need help. It's going to take another five years before we can say that the women at the provincial level are very much involved.

Lena Gallup

Lena Gallup's grandfather, a Metis known as "Sure Shot",
fled from Manitoba about 1870 after Riel's first uprising and established the Athabasca Transportation Company in Alberta. His son, Lena's father, carried on the business and she was born in an isolated trading post in Saskatchewan. Orphaned by the time she was five, she and her two sisters were raised by their Indian grandmother who supported them by trapping. Lena now lives in Calgary.

We lived in a tent at times, even in winter, and ate bannock, rabbits, and squirrels that grandmother snared. She knew a lot about herbs too and she gave them to us when we were ill. Grandmother was old and when I was seven we had to be sent to a mission school. The mission was on Lesser Slave Lake. The RCMP came to collect us with a dog team and took two of us to Fort McMurray. They missed our youngest sister – grandmother must have hidden her – and the police had to go all the way back.

School was a frightening world. We weren't allowed to speak Cree, that "savage tongue." It was all we knew although my father had been able to speak Cree, Chipewyan, French and English. For ten years life was hard: scrubbing floors (all mission girls develop calloused knees), catechism, prayers and group baths with a cold-water hose. Brrh! But there were happy times too: sliding on ice, riding farm horses and summer visits to beaches.

When I was a little girl I did think about becoming a nun but when I was 17, I went to work in a nursing home in Edmonton instead. That's where I discovered an aptitude for nursing that I think many native women have. I tried lots of jobs in the next few years, even worked as a salad chef at the Macdonald Hotel in Edmonton. Then I had TB and had to go to hospital. Later I trained as a nursing aide and worked in Edmonton and Calgary.

Since I married I have lived in Calgary. It was here that I joined the Indian community as an organizer and chaperone with a recreation group formed by a friend of mine. This led to an invitation to look after Indian students who came to the city for upgrading courses. I worked for Indian Affairs and was involved visiting reserves with the Blackfoot-Stony-Sarcee agency. Now I work only with urban Indians. I have been a director of the Calgary Indian Friendship Centre and a supervisor and guidance counsellor for native students. I believe strongly in government of Indians by Indians and I work closely with the Calgary Urban Treaty Indian Alliance. I am, for a second term, on the board of Indian News Media which operates Kainai News and the weekly *Blackfoot* and *Treaty No. 7* radio programs. Often I get asked to speak about problems of Indians in cities and for two years I coordinated and chaired a lecture series for the University of Calgary featuring prominent Canadian natives. All of this must have been the reason I was chosen for the Volunteer-of-the-Year award by city council.

Lately I have been spending more time with my family. I have a beautiful home and teenage children to look after. My life now is so very different to the years of my own childhood.

Gloria George

Born in Telkwa, British Columbia, Gloria George is the daughter of an hereditary chief. She is a member of the Grouse Clan of the Carrier tribe. Through her involvement with native organizations, Gloria has travelled extensively throughout the whole of Canada and has now become the first native woman to be elected national president of the Native Council of Canada. She became actively involved by organizing local groups near her home area in 1971, then was elected secretary-treasurer by acclamation to the provincial B.C. Association of Non-status Indians. By 1972, she was secretary-treasurer for the national association and two years later she was elected to the vice-president post. She became the national president in June 1975.

I think that native people in Canada today realize that certain individuals can carry out certain functions through their own sincerity and honesty. I believe this is why I was elected national president. Many people have asked me if I was elected because I was a woman since this was International Women's Year. My future was planned long before the United Nations declared an international year for women. I have a task to perform and that is to create new avenues for native people with the opportunities that are available to them. Through these resources, they can learn to help themselves.

My priority is to sensitize the general public so that they will understand what native people have contributed to Canadian history. I want to make them aware how native people live in their communities and how they function at the regional, provincial, territorial and national levels. Many native leaders across Canada recognize the fact that we are divided legally, socially, economically and psychologically. We want to eliminate these artificial definitions – status, non-status, registered, non-registered, treaty, non-treaty Indians, half-breeds and Metis. We want others to respect our own tribal, cultural and clan identity. These terms not only confuse the general public but also the native people who live in remote areas where they relate to one another as people of native ancestry. In the Northwest Territories they are now identifying themselves as the Dene people which means people of the land. Community leaders are saying we have to take a different stand. We have to get together on our common aims and objectives in order to work together.

Our culture has been eroded in language, spiritual beliefs, and self-identity. I use the term culture as a concept that applies to all indigenous people in Canada. Years ago, when children were sent to residential missionary schools, they were away from home ten months of the year. This

67 meant loss of language and identity with their parents and created the breakdown of family groups. A new educational process is taking place. We are evaluating who we are and identifying with our ancestors with pride. As a child, when we did something wrong, our mother or father would tell us a story which carried a message that did not affect us at the time. Later we recognized the meaning of the message: it is to respect those around us and respect ourselves.

There is a definite change taking place in the short period I've been involved. It sort of scares me to a certain extent. Native organizations are advancing rapidly and, as we learn from our mistakes, we are assisting these new groups with who, when and how to approach those who can help them. Cultural education and other special interest groups are evolving. We are going through a developmental stage with long-term objectives, economically, socially and culturally. Native people were always intelligent but this talent bank has been dormant too long. Part of our transition is to use these human resources. I feel quite strongly that the time is near when there will be a greater input from native women, especially if they exert pressure where necessary with respect to equal opportunities for their people. I am very proud of my native ancestry even though I am also part of another ancestry. I think when the general public recognizes the contributions we have made to the history of this country it will be a happy day for all of us. Then maybe we can say we are all Canadians. But, for some of us, it will be a long time before we can really say this with pride.

Rita Guiboche

In the 43 years of her life, Rita Guiboche has moved around Manitoba working as a nurse in sanitoriums, and across the country from James Bay to Vancouver. Now she lives in Camperville, Manitoba where she was born. She has been involved in organizing the Metis Women's Association, of which she is president, and in developing the Metis Academy. Rita has eight children but recently lost a young daughter to leukemia.

I have always been in some sort of organization, starting as first president of a teen club in Camperville. My school life was cut short at grade eight as that's as far as you could go in Camperville in those days. During the two years I spent in a sanitorium with tuberculosis, I finished grade nine by correspondence. After that I worked as a practical nurse and I think I have been in every sanitorium in Manitoba.

Being able to speak four languages; English, Cree, Saulteaux and a bit of French, has helped me to communicate with Metis women. I feel strongly that so many of them have been left behind. We accept non-status Indian women in our organization as they are sometimes rejected by Indian people if their children are Metis. The priority objective of our organization is to unite, educate, inform and activate Metis women in Manitoba to grow personally, socially, economically and politically. Another priority is to promote the well-being of Metis people in Metis communities. Therefore, we are promoting family planning and counselling programs among them. Society and the church has brainwashed men and women "to go forth and multiply." When the pill first came out, I encouraged women to take it. I guess this is when I started to break away from the church.

What most people don't realize is that we Metis are a very young nation, only about 200 years old, so our culture is new. Most other ethnic groups are thousands of years old. To my knowledge we're the youngest ethnic group in the world. Many people are confused about us.

69 We're not white and not Indian but part of both. In many ways, we have been rejected by both groups. I believe that individuals should be what they want to be and we're trying to help people to help themselves. Often we don't know about the society we're exposed to and, consequently, the Metis in remote rural areas and in urban areas have been left behind in the affluence of Canada.

The Manitoba Metis Federation, formed in 1967, is aimed at uniting Metis people and promoting greater interest in education and involvement in local organizations in hundreds of communities. It has done much to destroy the apathy and lethargy of many communities. The Metis Academy we're trying to set up here is to foster a greater awareness of Metis history and culture and to develop programs for young people to improve their knowledge and develop leadership skills. We're not trying to develop an elite group but to help all Metis society.

My husband and I have donated a large piece of land, close to the lake, where we hope to build a centre and museum to house all historical materials pertinent to Metis culture. A lack of knowledge of our own history has contributed to the negative self-concept many Metis people hold. We're a unique cultural group and have made a great contribution to Canada. If Metis people understand this it will reduce their frustrations and grievances with the present society and give them something to focus on. The Metis Women's Association is helping. Through our organization, Metis women are realizing their potential to work and live in today's world, equal to anybody else.

Vera Richards

first woman court worker in Winnipeg magistrate's court, she noticed that native women prisoners had a hard time and decided to help by joining the Manitoba Metis Federation and native women's groups. When the National Native Women's Association was formed, she was the acting chairman. Through her hobby of quilting, Vera has become an authority on traditional native patterns and hopes to open a shop when she retires.

At school we were judged by our achievements and, as I was top of my class, I was not thought of as an Indian. In high school, I couldn't attend regularly as we had to work to provide our clothes and books, and my father, who was an ex-history professor from the University of Toronto, took us out of school and taught us himself. He didn't want his kids in the school system anyway. He made us read the classics and at the time I thought it was boring but now I realize that it gave me a good background in the English language. It was when I tried to get a job with Winnipeg Electric driving a bus during the war that I was tagged as an Indian. I was told the colour of my skin would offend the public. So I was hired to work in the transit garage cleaning engines. That lasted three months: I was too small. So I was transferred to the office and worked there for 17 years.

Then I got a job in the Attorney General's office and was asked to go into the courtroom to interpret policy and procedures to native people. Seeing girls from the north who had been around an American army base and had grown super-sophisticated in some ways, yet were so disadvantaged and criticized in court, made me determined to

Vera Richards, born in Poplar Point, Manitoba, grew up completely isolated from any Indian community and did not realize she was part Cree until she went to work in Winnipeg. As the

71 find out all I could about native people. I identified with them.

I started going to native women's meetings and helped organize the Friendship Centre in Winnipeg. Before that, it seemed that other ethnic people had their own groups but native people did not. There were many ups and downs because the native people who were hired never had any business experience.

There was so much I had to learn about them. Because I have always had to struggle for survival, I'm quite aggressive. I used to be very trusting and thought everyone was honest but to survive among men, with government and with the vices people have, turns you into a bit of a different creature. What hit me hardest was to find out that people can do some pretty horrible things out of greed.

I really value the Indian religion which appreciates the elements and nature, things that make it possible to exist. People don't value their backgrounds the way they used to. My mother is very artistic. She taught us to sew and she really instilled the work ethic in us. There was no fooling around until you finished your work. It is different now when everybody just steps forth and asks for things.

I think native people are worse off now than when I started working in government years ago. I am quite vocal and very sure this is my country and I can live in it in a way I can enjoy. When I look at other native people and see that there is so little support for the things they would like to do, I feel I can save them a lot of hurdles I had to jump myself. I have always been an advocate of cleaning up your own backyard and this isn't happening.

Dakotas

Eva McKay

Eva McKay is the former president of the Manitoba Native Women's Association. In 1965, she helped start the Brandon Friendship Centre and lives on the Sioux Valley reserve in nearby Griswold. Eva proves that life can begin at 50.

I stayed home and raised my 12 children. Life was hard. Without education it's like being a blind person. I used to be bitter about white people and confused about what to believe. Then our house burned down. That was the turning point. I couldn't get any help. Government wouldn't listen. Suddenly I realized life had to change. Indian people have to help themselves. I didn't want the same thing to happen to anyone else. That was in 1959. The next year I became a band councillor, went to all sorts of meetings and did lots of volunteer jobs. Then I took leadership and sensitivity training and did some speaking at Brandon University about Indian religion.

Our young people have a conflict with Christianity and between Indian and white traditions. Our culture is something we must know about. Five years ago I went back to Indian spiritual beliefs and found new hope. Now I can see that, above everything, our Creator is here, around us. But each individual must choose. I want to help students know who they are so they don't get swallowed up in the white world. The two happiest days of my life were in 1974 when the native students at Brandon had a conference and asked me to be their representative mother – a mother to them all. I really, really enjoyed that as I felt I had been able to help some of them. Most of my work has been voluntary. In 1970, when I was 50, I got my

75 first pay cheque from the Manitoba Indian Brotherhood and I didn't know what to do with it.

Indian women of Manitoba now have a family health education program to help with family planning, alcoholism, drugs and VD. I accept family planning because unwanted children are no good. And alcohol; we can't be Indians if we consume alcohol. We must fight it. We all have to work together on common problems and not be separated by legal differences. On the reserve we have a women's club and handicraft association but something I really want to get is a swimming pool. We need more recreation to bring families together in ways other than drinking.

I have learned to take the ups with the downs and if I get sick and unable to work, I will be satisfied that I have done some good.

Martha Tawiyaka

Martha Tawiyaka, a tiny Dakota woman less than five feet
tall, lives alone in a red and white house on the Standing
Buffalo reserve in southern Saskatchewan. Now 100 years old,
she can recall the time when, as a child of four, she came over
the border with her parents in 1881.

I can remember Sitting Bull put on a Ghost dance when he
and his band camped here. We girls went to see it. During
the day they danced the Pow-wow. At night they wore
white clothing and masks. They looked like ghosts. The
Dakota and Cree were enemies and we had to run away
from Duck Lake to avoid being in the war. My aunt cried,
then started to cook. Soon the rest of the family came in a
Red River cart. I can remember the Mounties and the
soldiers when they were camped at Fort Qu'Appelle before
the march to Duck Lake.

I like it here on the reserve. My grandsons farm all
around here. The Dakota up here are neat and keep their
yards clean but in the States they have trash piles right outside the door. The lake here used to be clear and sweet
smelling the year round, now it is green and smells bad all
summer. We used to drink from the lake when I was young.
My late husband was a "thunder dreamer." He used to fill
a pipe before a storm and ask the thunders to come quietly.
Before a fierce storm the thunder would shout "whoo" to
let him know lightning was going to strike. My husband
was an Indian doctor. He blew on people. I was a midwife
and made good medicines. I used to be a great dancer too,
before my husband died.

I went to school when I was seven and stayed 12 years. I liked it there with the Sisters. One time they took me with them to Winnipeg to a religious retreat. No one was allowed to speak. I liked it. I wanted to be a nun but my father took me out of school when he heard of that. I learned to tan hides and sew with sinew. I can make porcupine quillwork too.

I like to eat porcupine. To cook one, you boil it a few minutes first, then bake it. I still dry venison and make pemmican. I never eat garlic, bologna, eggs or store-bought bread. I eat venison, duck and rabbit. Duck eggs are good. I never drink coffee, only tea. If you ask me what is most different about young people today and young people when I grew up, I would say this: today's young people have no respect.

Lorraine Yuzicapi

Lorraine Yuzicapi lives near Regina on a farm that is part of the 11-acre Standing Buffalo reserve where she grew up. In the last few years, the reserve has had a housing improvement program and developed a new recreation club and tourist resort. Lorraine has been involved in all these activities.

Everybody had a job to do on the farm, looking after the horses, feeding the chickens and watering the chickens. I had four brothers and eight sisters and used to go hunting with the boys. My parents come from different Dakota councils. My father is a Santee of the Sisseton-Wahpeton and my mother is a Teton of the Oglala council. They spoke different dialects. My mother claimed that hers was a higher class than Daddy's. Very few little kids speak Sioux now but it's really important to the culture and I am teaching it in school.

When I was at school I was good at cooking and sewing and was asked to teach them, but I had all sorts of jobs; nurses' aide, cooking in a motel, driving a van and when we had time, we farmed. For a time I worked for the Saskatchewan Indian Women's Association organizing women in the area, then I went back to work on the reserve.

In the early seventies, our reserve was behind all the others. Then we got a LIP program started and now the reserve is going great guns. I was project manager for a housing improvement program and was on the band council. We laid down strict rules about working hours for the men. We had a group of 15 men and five women. The men cut wood and fixed houses and the women sewed

79 blankets and curtains for people in need. Over the winter we installed furnaces in 32 houses and supplied 60 homes with wood and seven homes with running water and had a truck from town for other water. Now we are taking over our own housing and road repairs. One summer when I coordinated a work opportunity program, we hired men on welfare and formed a recreation club. I was also on the school committee but had to quit as it was too much with all the other things.

I am committed to the Pow-wow committee. Sioux Pow-wows are important. Another thing that is important is the handicrafts co-op. We have a central marketing scheme and Ottawa sends things we make to other countries. One really exciting project is our tourist resort – a commerical venture. Maybe it will take five to ten years to complete but we have started winterizing cabins on the lake, building a store and boating area and ramps. Then we are going to build a ski hill, trailer camp area and a covered rink. This involves the community and gives people jobs. I have worked ever since I can remember. I have two kids but there wasn't time to have any more. There is so much to do.

Iroquois

Marlene Castellano

Marlene Castellano, like other Mohawks of Quinte Bay, is proud of her tribe. She maintains close ties with the Tyendinaga reserve where she was born. Both her grandfathers were chiefs on the reserve and her parents still live there. After taking her B.A. and a Master's degree in social work, Marlene faced the difficult choice between marriage and her commitment to work for Indian people. She did both and is now assistant professor of native studies at Trent University, Peterborough, Ontario.

Until I went to university I had no exposure to our history. Being Mohawk had been a personal thing not connected with any sense of tradition. Mohawks were familiar. They were my people. To go off the reserve meant to go among strangers, and there was a lot of anxiety involved with that. In school when I learned about the savage Iroquois and how they slaughtered the brave pioneers and priests, I made no connection between the text books and the Mohawks of which I was one. But at university, people began to ask questions about my Indianness and I realized

that I had been socialized into an identity that totally ignored my heritage and history. This was the beginning of my conscious efforts to sort out what it means to me to be an Indian in modern society.

There was never any question in my mind that I wanted to work with my own people and when I finished my first year of social work training I went back to live on the reserve and worked with the local Children's Aid Society. I wanted to relate the theoretical things I was learning to real life situations. Then I went to Toronto to complete my Master's degree and afterwards to Winnipeg. There I was involved with the Indian-Metis Friendship Centre during its first year and I worked with the Winnipeg Children's Aid Society in the family service department.

That year I had to make a very difficult decision. I had met a man with whom I felt I could make a very good life but to do that meant abandoning my commitment to be a banner-carrier for Indian people. At the age of 25 with a Master's degree, there were a lot of doors open to me and opportunities to do things that hadn't been done before. I chose to do the thing that was right for me personally. I got married and had four sons and for the next ten years my primary role was that of a homemaker and mother. As it turned out, it was the right thing for my commitment to Indian people as well. My family now provides a base of emotional support and stability, the real foundation for the demanding job of teaching and counselling young people at Trent.

Fifteen years ago, when I was in Winnipeg, I was being asked to participate in conferences, give interviews to

83 television and newspapers and undertake a variety of exciting jobs. The reason I did not stay with it was that I was so alone, away from my reserve, my tribe, my family. There was nobody there who really shared the kinds of things I was going through. Nobody who could understand. The generation I am in had to make a choice, either/or, because at that time society did not provide the spaces for women to both have a job and a family. Now that it has been recognized that women's talents are very much needed for some of the important jobs in society, young women are not required to make that choice any more.

I think that if you are going to be in a position to respond to other people's needs, then you need support and understanding in your own life. As it turned out, I have the best of both worlds – a very happy family and an interesting job working for native people. I need my tribe and now I have my own to carry around with me.

Since I have been at Trent, involved with Indian young people trying to find their place in society, and also teaching non-native students who are interested in learning about us, I realize what great blanks there are in Indian history. The history of Canada is going to have to be rewritten to include the role of native people and show we were not just savages prancing around the pallisades. We were one of the founding groups of the Canadian nation. There is a great deal to be done but I find you cannot make a long-term plan; just be prepared to do the most useful thing that is open to you now – and things have a way of snowballing.

June Delisle

June Delisle was born on the Caughnawaga reserve near Montreal where she has lived all her life. She is a member of the Bear clan of the Mohawk tribe within the Six Nations Iroquois Confederacy. She is the Administrator of the Kateri Memorial Hospital Center on the reserve and an active member of the Board of Directors. Other involvement in community activities involved working with teen-agers and the local Homemakers Club. Her greatest influence and encouragement for the work she is doing came from her parents. Continued support from other members of her family, particularly her brothers, has taught her the importance of what it means to be an Indian.

My father, being Chief of the band at one time, was always involved in Indian work. My grandfather was Chief and so was my great grandfather. More recently my brother also became Band Chief. I am sure what they felt was gained from our ancestors. They were glad that I had a chance to get an education and since I enjoyed school they did not have to convince me to stay. I wish they had

more education than I had but that was something I could not do anything about. Another influence was my big brother who was very patient with me in school work and spent many hours by lamplight telling me why things were so important and why I should learn. I spent 17 and a half years working in Montreal commuting from the reserve. The people I worked with accepted me not only because I was an Indian but I had the ability to express myself openly as I was taught to do at home.

I always felt that there was something I had to do that needed to be done. Ten years ago the opportunity came for me to work on the reserve. I became involved in the local hospital as a bookkeeper and worked my way to the administrator's position. I believe that my greatest contribution to my community has been my interest in what was happening to the health and welfare of the people on the reserve. It was very important to me that they get the best medical care possible. I became concerned about the kinds of doctors and nurses we had, the kind of medications the people were getting as inpatients and outpatients and so on. One of the important things a hospital always needs is money. Giving talks to raise funds, I became involved in getting support from people at the local level and in the city of Montreal.

When I came back to work on the reserve I was told, "June, don't rock the boat," but I love rocking the boat and I'll continue to rock it because I think that in order to get things done you have to make waves. There are many frustrations in working among your people but you have to be able to put up with them. You have to know

85 how to fight for what you think your people need as Indians. Sometimes I get involved at our local level of government where I feel I have to put up a good fight because it means something better for my people. Sometimes I may be wrong but I've got to at least prove that I am either right or wrong.

Lately I have been doing some work with the Indians of Quebec Association on better health conditions for our people throughout the province. I know it is important that something be done in this area because of the letters and phone calls I get from those who are not aware of what is available to them. I think one of the drawbacks right now is communication among Indians, whether it be on the reserve, provincial or national level. In Quebec we have a language problem. Thirty per cent of the Indian people speak French as their second language. This, too, has to be resolved.

About the future? I think it is necessary that the young people be made to understand the importance of getting an education. Not simply an academic education but to help them understand what their way of life was and to do all we can to help them make the choice of what their life should be. I think it is important that we, as Indian people, should work together and decide what our future should be. We must take over and manage our own affairs and learn to control our own destiny. I don't know if people really understand what it is like to be an Indian today and what an Indian can do. To me, being Indian is my right but to do something about those rights is up to me as an individual.

Kitty Maracle

Kitty Maracle, a Cayuga born on the Six Nations reserve, now lives in Vancouver and is the past-president of the B.C. Native Women's Society. For some years she lived in Rochester, New York, raising 12 children, seven of them her own. Kitty believes Indian culture can only be maintained by keeping a land base and language. She thinks the question of status is not widely understood and the section of the Indian Act relating to status has divided people and destroyed family structure.

I find that most Indian women and men are hung up emotionally about the status question. Many of them do not realize that it was not their decision to cast out Indian women or to accept white women as Indians. The Indian Act was legislation written by white men. I can understand the government trying to keep the feeling going that "Oh, it's just those non-status women who want to bring their white men back." But that's not looking at facts. Marriage is not the only way you can lose status and it's not just women who are losing it but men too. When the man signs off, his wife and kids have no choice but to lose automatically. So many full-blood Indians are being removed from the register. Now young girls are saying, "I'm not going to get married because I'm afraid of losing status," and they are shacking up. If the girls have been raised to respect their parents, just think how awful it is for all of them, this rejection between the girls and their parents and all because a legal technicality exists.

White women have become status Indians and have borne half-breed children and these half-Indians, quarter-Indians, are the ones now making decisions about what happens to Indian people. Training and teaching children is the role of the woman but no white woman can teach our culture, our heritage.

I think the question of status is just a red-herring being dragged in front of Indian people and I would like to see our organizations really fight to have that clause taken out of the Indian Act. Then more time can be spent on finding solutions to other problems like land claims. If native people lose their land and language, all is lost and we will

87   disappear. The Six Nations have been aware of white people for four or five hundred years and have seen what has happened to our own people.

There is lots we can do for ourselves. In Rochester, my husband and I ran a successful construction firm and hired nearly all Indians. We trained many to become carpenters and some of them now operate their own construction business. We formed an organization to get Indian people involved in sports and started a hockey club. The first people on the ice were hefty, known-drunks – nobody had thought they could do something like this. They took the inter-city championship that year and every years since! In Vancouver, some of us have formed a native consulting firm and a non-profit housing organization to buy houses to rent to Indians in urban centres, students, poor people, at a price they can afford to pay even though they're on welfare. I've owned and operated a native arts and crafts shop in Vancouver and am involved with many native organizations, dancing in the Indian War Dance Club and working with the B.C. Association of Non-status Indians.

Thoughts about losing our culture are always in my mind and heart and keep driving me on in my involvement. We can't change yesterday but we can start today and change tomorrow.

Kahn-Tineta Miller

One of nine children, Kahn-Tineta's name became famous across Canada in the sixties as a high fashion model in Montreal and Toronto. A Mohawk brought up on the Caughnawaga reserve, she travelled throughout North America and parts of Europe giving her outspoken views on Indian issues. She is a devoted supporter of the Long House, the traditional religion of the Iroquois.

I became involved over 12 years ago through writing and speaking. I was considered an activist and was involved in the beginnings of some associations like the National Indian Council which no longer exists and which I felt was not serving the best interest of Indians. My major contribution at that time was to focus public awareness and attention on the fact that Indians did exist, that we had legal rights and many social, economic and cultural problems in dealing with the world around us. I believe I was successful in doing just that. During my year of law studies at McGill University, I took on an important legal case involving the eviction of my own sister from the Caughnawaga reserve for marrying a non-Indian. It was a test case and before it got to the Federal Court of Canada she moved off the reserve. I'm glad to say she has now re-married a status Indian and is living on the Caughnawaga reserve. We are now the best of friends. This spurred other activities in connection with the rights of these former Indian women who marry non-Indians.

In my opinion, the Indian Act will not be changed substantially as it reflects the general feelings of Indian people. The only views being expressed on this issue are by these women who would like to have both worlds. Their retaining their status will damage the rights of Indians.

While I was advocating that Indians should not use birth control with the belief that there should be more Indians in Canada, I started to have my own children. I now have five children. The first three I had without the benefit of marriage. Because of my belief in the institution of marriage I did marry the father of my children but it did not work out so I have taken another course of action.

In the past, many of we Indians devoted much time and effort working on behalf of Indians and I think we accomplished a great deal in our own way without the aid of government-financed associations. These newly formed associations and Friendship Centres throughout Canada, supported by the government, started a lot of activities but, in my opinion, on the whole they have not advanced the first people. They have said much, they have criticized a great deal and they have made many suggestions. Mostly this tactic has led to rising expectations among Indians and half-breeds and false expectations of Indians by white people. I doubt that half-breeds will ever have the same rights as Indians. It's just too expensive. In the future there must be a complete separation of half-breed and Indian activities.

Land claims have come forward, disputes over hunting, fishing and treaty rights are being dealt with in courts. Mind you, I think some court actions are promoted mainly for the benefit of lawyers and promoters exploiting Indian people and the government.

The original reasons for legislating the Indian Act was

89　to protect our people so they would survive in a world that had completely changed. It separated Indians from other people. It protected Indian lands because Indians do not really have a feeling of possessiveness. They are not materialistic. Further, the Indian Act is basically legislation that must be there to protect Indians from themselves. What I see ahead is Indians demanding enforcement of the Indian Act, treaties and other legislation which protects Indians. Over the years I've been very critical of the Department of Indian and Northern Affairs so, two years ago, I decided to work for them to see if I could effect some changes. I believe we must protect the department and make sure it serves us. We may never see whether my ideas permeated the department. What is needed is right-thinking, experienced people in key policy-making positions. As long as policies are being decided by people who do not know the subject but are just passing through the department, there will never be any change.

One of our main problems over the years is that we have not developed enough outstanding Indian leaders. In some communities potential leaders have been eliminated because Indian people are still operating on a communal basis where everyone is considered equal. My studies over the years have strengthened the idea that the Indian will always continue to have a communal identity and operate from communal instincts. For this reason many government programs which are oriented to development of the individual are not successful. It creates conflicts which they cannot overcome. The government is reaching a stalemate: they are spending enormous sums and having less success. At the same time, we are losing some very outstanding Indians who are dying either of stress, heart attacks, accidents or suicides.

Educational programs should be geared to a new kind of training, to the kinds of pressures the Indian character can cope with in order to function in this world. There has to be an emphasis on Indian identity, not a pseudo-identity like running around wearing head bands. Indians themselves must become aware of their strong and weak characteristics. This means the imposition, right from birth, of the right kind of program which will enable Indians to cope with pressures of life around them and to fit in as Indians.

91

Odsïg 61

Daphne Odjig Beavon

Daphne Odjig Beavon is a member of the Odawa tribe of the Three Fires Confederacy. She is a successful artist whose paintings were bought by the National Museum of Man in Ottawa and were on display in the Canadian pavilion at Expo '70 in Japan. She has had many international exhibitions. Recently she opened her own gallery and native art shop in Winnipeg to encourage other Indian artists. She was born on the Wikwemikong reserve in Ontario.

I have always painted as did my father and grandfather. They encouraged me from the time I was a little girl living on the reserve where my family farmed. We knew what hard work was. I had to milk cows before I went to school and after I came home. I taught myself to paint and started by illustrating the legends my grandparents used to tell me. I didn't get any help from school; in fact, art was suppressed there. After I left the reserve I got married and went to live in British Columbia. That's where I was first able to sell my art.

Even art schools can't teach art but what they can do is to provide useful technical background so that an artist can extend his own experience and use new materials. Every artist has his own mental image to portray and has to learn to use materials his own way. I love to experiment and I think this is the only way to develop and to retain an individuality in your work. Paint is not my only medium; I have used all kinds of natural materials such as nuts, pine cones, wild rice, bird's feathers and beads for collages. My art has progressed through many different stages because I have been learning through my own experiments. What is really important to me at the moment is to continue to develop as an artist.

There is no one way for any artist. Life is a constant search for identity and that is all part of your own ethnic background. All my work is essentially Indian though it has taken many different forms. When I went to live in northern Manitoba I realized that the old pioneer way of life on Indian reserves was slowly dying out so I tried to capture some of it with pen and ink drawings. These were

93 real people and actual places which I hope will live for ever through the medium of art. A lot of my work is abstract, figments of my imagination, and recently I have written and illustrated a series of children's books, *Little Legends for Little People,* about the adventures of an Indian spirit-man.

I believe the New Odjig Warehouse gallery of native art and native craft shop in downtown Winnipeg is the only gallery totally owned and operated by native people. It is somewhere for artists to exhibit their works without paying heavy fees or commissions. If someone had given me that chance ten years ago I would have been very happy. A variety of art forms are exhibited here and the artists come from many different backgrounds.

We want to compete in the world as artists, not just as Indian artists. Although I am proud to be Indian, I feel fortunate that I have a medium through which I can speak to Indian and non-Indian people alike. I always knew I had to paint but it took me years before I could feel secure and at peace with myself, psychologically and spiritually. I believe that our lives are pre-determined but it's up to you to do something about it. I know just how tough it is being an artist and I had to develop that will to better myself. That didn't come easily. I sign my work Odjig which is my maiden name and means the animal known as the fisher.

Jeannette Corbière-Lavell

Jeannette Corbière-Lavell, an Ojibway, left her home on the Wikwemikong reserve in Ontario on Manitoulin Island to seek employment. In Toronto she worked for a while as an executive secretary and from there went on to social work at the Canadian Indian Centre of Toronto. In 1965, Jeannette was selected as Indian Princess Canada. She was also employed by the Company of Young Canadians and travelled extensively across Canada working with native communities. Presently she is president of Nishnawbe Institute and Anduhyaun Inc., the latter a residence for native women in the city of Toronto. She is one of the founding members of the Ontario Native Women's Association, has been its president for two terms, and recently was elected as one of the vice-presidents of the Native Women's Association of Canada. She also studied for and received her teaching certificate after a number of years away from school. In 1970, Jeannette lost her legal status as an Indian person through marriage. She questioned this through a court of law and lost in the County Court, won in the Federal Court of Appeal, but lost again when it was appealed to the Supreme Court of Canada by the Attorney-General.

It was a very frustrating time as I was criticized by Indians and non-Indians alike. It was really a personal issue which developed into something the whole country got involved in.

Many people realized the significance of this issue. Through the Bill of Rights, Canadians are entitled to the *protection* of the law, regardless of race, sex, creed, etc. This means, in my case, that I was entitled to the protection of my legal status as an Indian person. Misinformation directly from the Department of Indian and Northern Affairs and mishandling by the media caused a lot of unnecessary confusion during the case. In County Court the judge refused to listen to what I had to say. He believed that I was better off marrying a white man. In fact, according to his readings, this was the thinking of all intelligent native people. He could not understand why I felt so strongly that I had as much right to my own nationality as anyone else. At the Federal Court of Appeal, there was no question about it. All three judges felt that I was being discriminated against as this particular section of the Indian Act applied only to Indian women and not Indian men. The Attorney-General's department appealed my victory to the Supreme Court of Canada, no doubt due to pressure from the Department of Indian Affairs and Northern Development and, sad to say, I lost by one vote. At first I was a little disillusioned about the whole system of justice and the reaction of Indians and non-Indians alike. Not only was this a legal loss but I felt it was also contrary to our traditional *values* of recognition and respect for each other.

Thinking about it now, I still feel it was a victory and worth all the worry and anxiety it produced because now native people as well as our political native organizations are looking at the whole question of Indian status and membership. This in itself is one step in the right direction. Changes will have to be made in the Indian Act. It cannot be allowed to remain as it is and I feel that all this will be worthwhile. In the Ontario Native Women's Associ-

95   ation we stress unity instead of the divisions imposed on us by the government. We recognize all women of native ancestry and we work together on the priorities that we have established. I believe that if we, as native people, all recognized and supported each other, we would have a lot more bargaining power with the government. Right now, we are allowing ourselves to be divided and consequently we are being conquered.

Nishnawbe Institute was founded by a group of native people of various backgrounds who were interested in native culture and its relevance to present way of life. It has developed and supported a number of projects one of which is the Indian Ecumenical Conference held annually on the Stoney Reserve in Morley, Alberta.

The Indian Ecumenical Conference brings together about five thousand native people from all over North America in a week-long gathering with spiritual leaders and medicine people. Here, our native people come together to pray, fast, dance and talk about the significance of our own spiritual beliefs and their influence. Young and old attend the conference, and there seems to be an increase in better communication between young people and spiritual elders. From the conference, we've found out that our native women have so much to offer and this had not been recognized before. Elderly native women have a lot of knowledge and wisdom which we have neglected to use and which has almost been forgotten. They know of medicines, nutrition, care of children, and a way of living which would be more relevant to us as a native people. They are the last survivors of our traditional way of life

as native women. Especially now we, as native people, need this wisdom and understanding.

In the past few years, we have seen native women's organizations develop and become more active in dealing with issues which affect them and their communities. As native women we are involved in the day-to-day existence and improvement of our communities through our homes and families, consequently we are interested in action rather than talk.

Dorothy Francis

Dorothy Francis, born in 1912, is a Saulteaux from the Waywayseecappo reserve in Manitoba. Her Indian name is Maqua Beak. She was raised with a strong awareness of her culture and has been involved in many projects which have encouraged her people to remember the great love and spiritual understanding that are part of Indian culture. In 1932, Dorothy married Joe Francis from the Kahkewistahow reserve in Broadview, Saskatchewan. Together they raised nine children and there are now 33 grandchildren and two great-grandchildren. Joe Francis died on July 25, 1974. She worked for many years with the Federation of Saskatchewan Indians and was appointed to the National Indian Arts and Crafts Advisory Committee as Saskatchewan's representative. She became the committee's chairperson in 1974. In 1964, Chatelaine Magazine awarded Dorothy the Gold Key Award for service to her people.

When I was a child I lived with my grandmother in a log cabin and she taught me about the crafts of our people and our culture. I spoke only Saulteaux till the age of seven when a white couple drove up to our home in a buggy and took me away to the Birtle Indian Residential School.

I can remember that the people on the reserve had a great respect for life and were deeply spiritual. Many feasts of thanksgiving and songs and dances celebrating life took place. We have so much culture that has nearly been lost. If you say that to some people, they won't know what you're talking about. Some Indian people don't know which way to go. They have never learned. A lot of young people have never had a chance to develop. We should go hand-in-hand with our fellow men trying to understand and identify ourselves and portray a good picture of our people. It took me a long time to find out what it was all about.

I was fighting between two cultures. My own religion had been called paganism. That did not make any sense when I knew my people had this great love and understanding for family. With so much love, how could they be bad? They tell you that our religion is not right but I feel that all good teachings come from the same source, one God and one mankind. When you respect, love, honour and obey the Creator you are surrounded by vibrations and feelings of love. Sometimes we see beauty, sometimes ugliness. That is the Creator's way of making us learn. We must be strong and make our own decisions. Knowledge of how to survive makes you what you are. It took me a long time to learn but now it can never be put aside.

I have spent many years of my life promoting Indian culture, particularly arts and crafts. In the early sixties my family and I moved to Winnipeg where I became associated with the Indian Friendship Centre. I was eventually hired to manage the first arts and crafts program for the centre and later was offered a job as a family counsellor. I helped set up the first Winnipeg Pow-wow Club and, with the assistance of Nan Shipley, did a series of television programs telling Indian stories for children. In the late sixties I moved to Regina and started the Indian Cultural Club and became a member of the Saskatchewan Provincial Arts Board. I also worked for the CBC on an Indian program, "North Country Fair", acting as hostess, speaking English and Saulteaux on the air. While in Regina I introduced an Indian lullaby to the Saskatchewan Folklore Society through Mrs. Barbara Cass-Beggs and wrote Indian legends with the help of Muriel Clipsham.

In 1967, I travelled around schools in Alberta, Saskatchewan and Manitoba with a group of dancers and storytellers as part of a centennial project. We explained the meaning of dance steps and movements and the philosophy of Indian beliefs and legends which many people have lost. It was then that my late husband and I were invited to dine with the Queen. That was one of the highlights of our lives.

My aim in life is to pass on our own precious Indian religious teachings and heritage. It is obvious that society around us is in chaos with all its injustice and destruction. We must do all we can to educate ourselves about our own religion. We must know God and worship Him so we can love and work for our fellow men and be properly guided and proud of our identity. One of my objectives in life is to help people on reserves find out what it really means to be an Indian in a deep spiritual sense. Then I think we will have a great role to play in helping bring out unity of mankind and making a happier and better world to live in.

Irene Hoff

In 1974, after more than 32 years working in Ottawa for the federal government, Irene Hoff retired. Irene, an Abenaki woman, returned to the Odanak reserve near Trois Rivières, Quebec where she was born. After attending business college in

Ottawa, Irene had qualified for civil service employment and had begun work in Air Force headquarters. During the war she served overseas with the St. John Ambulance Brigade then, returning to Canada, she joined the Department of Indian and Northern Affairs as one of the first Indian employees. She served in the Canadian Army Women's Corps militia for 11 years and is believed to have been the first Canadian Indian woman to receive a commission.

My early years in the Department of Indian Affairs were very enjoyable and fruitful, both in acquiring knowledge and financially. I feel that those of us who were employed in the department paved the way for future employment of native people. At that time, we had to qualify for entry into the civil service in the same manner as other persons and earn promotion as well. Much has been said and discussed about the present native employment in the department but I firmly believe that a person should be employed on the basis of qualification and not on the basis of Indian background alone. When I started to work there it was much, much smaller and I think the employees were more interested in each other and in the Indian people who came in. It was more of a family. But I think the department fell down a lot in the past because they didn't have the money they have now.

Now it has grown into such a large organization and they are too generous with the money. Large sums of money are provided to Indian organizations and band councils across the country and this is too much financial

99 responsibility without proper training, supervision or accountability. The department is always talking about being able to communicate with people but they don't do that today. They just can't do it because it is a great big machine and nobody is really interested in the employees, in Indian people. Also, there is poor communication between council and band members and this allows for poor administration.

The status of Indian women is another matter on which, like many others, I have very strong feelings. Since I retired I have been able to attend council meetings. Nothing irks me more than to see non-Indian women who have acquired Indian status through marriage, sitting on band councils, or monopolizing the floor at meetings, while Indian women married to non-Indians lose their rights to be elected and to participate in band affairs. This is a difficult matter, of course, but it should, and must, be resolved.

In the final analysis, we native people must strive to work out our own destiny as one and not be divided as we are now. No one can do that for us but it is necessary to have understanding, cooperation and communication not only with the Department of Indian and Northern Affairs and the non-Indian society, but most of all with our fellow native people across this vast country of ours. I never thought, like a lot of people do, that the government owed me a living. I don't think that anybody owes anyone anything. That's something you have to work out for yourself.

Elsie Knott

grocery store and post office, driving the school bus, starting a day-care centre and Pow-wow, as well as being a Sunday school superintendent, girl guide leader and scout and cub master. Now 53, she is a life senator of the Union of Ontario Indians.

The year 1952 was when politics started in for Indian women. That was the first time women were able to run for office or to vote. I was elected chief and stayed chief for eight years. I thought I'd give up politics but some people put my name up for counsellor without me knowing. I got more votes than all the men. I think women can be good in politics. They are more demanding. Everyone helps a woman. You can get people behind you if they think there is something good going on.

We have 700 members but some of them are away from the reserve. About four to five hundred live here. People are coming back on account of the housing. It's a lot cheaper than in the city.

When I went to school there was no mention of high school. We stopped after grade eight. The first year I became chief, five students wanted to go to high school real bad but the reserve was six or seven miles from the highway and there was a problem over transportation. We got one of the boys to take them but he got fed up after just one morning and quit. I said I would drive them until they got somebody else if it was important to them. I guess they never found anyone else because that was 22 years ago and I'm still driving them. When others saw those children going to school, they wanted to go too. The

Elsie Knott, an Ojibway of Curve Lake reserve in Ontario, was the first woman Chief to be elected in Canada. She was married at 15 and had three children by the time she was 20. Always active in the community, Elsie has been involved in running the

101 next year I had 29 and now there are 130. We have two 78-passenger buses. I drive one and my daughter drives the other. All I had at first was an old van with no seats so we put car seats on the floor. I really wanted those children to get a better education. Driving the bus is hard work and I have to take a test every two years now that I'm over 50, but I like to keep busy.

Since we started all this I've seen a lot of changes. When I first took them they were talking Indian, now they don't understand it. All those below the age of 25, they've lost it. I think it's terrible. I did try to have Ojibway classes for three or four years but now I'm so busy belonging to different organizations. The children like singing in Indian even though they can't speak it, can't make a sentence. I translated 14 songs for them to sing at concerts at Christmas. Some of them are happy they're Indians but they lose it in school. That's what I think. It's maybe the history books. They seem to make an image of the Indian that he's wild and dirty, then the white students sitting beside them think they are like that so Indian students want to forget they're Indian.

There are about 25 children in the day-care centre looked after by an Indian supervisor, a cook, three other women and one white girl. She's just like an Indian now, she likes it so well. Mothers go out working and leave their children there in the mornings. They get their meals and we don't charge anything. We have a reserve kindergarten and grades one and two. Children really have it good now and lots of them are going to college.

Helen Martin

Helen Martin, a Micmac of Sydney, Nova Scotia, has organized native women's groups throughout the province and helped form the Micmac Cultural Institute. Without any formal education, as she spent 12 years of her childhood in hospital, Helen learned to read and write English only as an adult. She finds common sense is more important than education for women wanting to work in their communities and that men on reserves are helpful once they understand what women are trying to do.

It was a very shocking experience for me when I went to hospital in Halifax. I was only two. My father and mother visited me often but we had to talk to each other through an open window. They spoke in Micmac and when I answered in English they worried that I would lose my language. When I left the hospital it was like leaving home.

My father said I had to learn to work and be independent so, when I was 18, I went to Truro and worked in a hotel. I had a burning desire to be able to read and write and to express my thoughts but my knowledge of English was limited and the Micmac language lacked English equivalents. When I thought of the humiliating incidents that happened to me and the times whites called me simple, I got discouraged and felt that I could do nothing for myself or my race. Then I met a non-Indian who found somebody to teach me to read and write in English. I paid my own tuition fee and I started writing about the Micmacs. Then I was asked to speak about my people to Kiwanis and other clubs.

We didn't have education in Nova Scotia at that time, only Indian day schools up to grade eight. There was no way of getting into high school because they wouldn't accept an Indian. My father was a chief for 42 years and my family had chiefs way back since 1802 so I ran for chief and lost out by three votes, because I was a woman, I guess.

When I lost my husband I just didn't know what to do and was really depressed. I had no income and living in an old abandoned place with no lights or water. Then one day someone was going around talking about an election that night to select someone to go to Alberta on meetings. I got elected, then nearly backed down as I'd never been on an airplane, but I said to myself, "I'm only going to die once." When I got to the meeting, I heard other women talking and said to myself, "My goodness, they have a marvellous education. They know what they're talking about." I was elected to be on a steering committee and I didn't know what I was steering so I took my dictionary out and got the idea. Back home I called a women's meeting and told them what I had heard in Alberta. They just

103 looked at me and didn't say a word. When I said, "Do you want to get organized provincially?" everybody put up their hands.

During our founding conference the native women of Nova Scotia found that the Micmac people were losing their Indian culture and I kept stressing that the women had to do something to bring it back. We had workshops and I urged them to run for councillors so they weren't left out of band meetings. We got a lot of help from our men. It was a learning experience for them too. Over this "status – non-status" thing, the women thought the white men were going to take over our reserves and throw us out on the streets so our organization was bogging down. Then I got ten students to work for us from the Student Community Service Program. They really did a marvellous job. I gave them information about women's associations and they got it into every reserve and community. After that the women had less fear. It really worked.

I began to organize eight reserves and they are still developing and doing things on their own. We asked them, "Are you not proud that you are Indian people?" and said "We don't want to lose our language." Now we have the Micmac Cultural Institute and our children will be learning the language in schools. Most reserves have a Micmac choir and do a lot of arts and crafts. After this experience I feel that if a woman wants to do something it is not necessary to have a high education, just plain common sense. You can see the problems and hear them . . . then you have to get a group together and help each other to do something. This is how I feel.

Alanis Obomsawin

Alanis Obomsawin, an Abenaki woman from the Odanak reserve in Quebec, became well known through her story-telling and singing and was invited to work at the National Film Board. Her work has made it possible for native people to communicate in a unique way. With cameras and tape-recorders she helps old people and children to listen to each other. Her film strips on Indian life are used all over the world. Alanis has special respect for old people, children and animals. She fears that individuals who are given power often grow ugly unless they use it to help other people.

I grew up with old people. They were very strong, beautiful people and had a way of thinking, of living and of being which was very good. I looked up to them and as I grew older I wanted so much to be like them. It is only today that I realize how fortunate I was and what they meant to me. I feel their presence: I don't feel alone.

Stories and songs were always a part of me but when, in the sixties, someone asked me to sing in a concert in New York, I didn't really want to. I was frightened but finally I accepted and that was the beginning of my sharing with people of all races. What I brought to them was a present from our people of long ago. This was not always understood but as time went by I had the feeling that people were really listening.

Since my main interest is children, I have tried to concentrate in touring schools, summer camps and generally places where children go. I have given concerts for adults in museums, art centres, folk festivals and old people's homes. I have travelled to many native communities all across the country to sing and play with children.

When a child is born, it is like a miracle and as he grows up, his needs are very basic. He must have someone strong and honest close to him. If this person happens to be a parent so much the better because a child in his early behavior always tries to copy his parents or the person close to him. It was the custom of our people to tell children stories and songs. Many stories were told and most of them were about animals because the best friends of our people were the animals.

A child would listen and through the stories he would decide which animal he would take his morals from. A child was free to develop his own mind, therefore would create his own discipline in the times to come.

When I was nine we moved from the reserve and went to live in Trois Rivières. It was a very difficult time, a discovery of things I didn't know that were ugly and bad.

When I slept, that was my best time because I had all my dreams, all my animals, a life of my own. I guess they formed my own beliefs and way of expressing myself. I really believe that when I die I will come back as an animal and will be very happy.

In all my dreams, we have protected one another; I feel I am them and they are me.

I feel that people of my age have witnessed and been through many painful changes and it's very difficult for many of us to survive through these changes.

I get very upset at the greediness of people. It is difficult to admit that some of these people are our own people.

105　To have power can be very useful and meaningful but if abused it can be very corrupting.

A few years ago I was asked by the National Film Board to be an advisor on a film about native people. That proved to be difficult because my advice was not necessarily followed and I worried that Indian people were being used.

After I was asked to make a film of my own, I went to a residential school at Moose Factory and I stayed with the children. I would tell stories and would go into the dormitories to sing for the kids before they went to sleep. The staff got angry; they didn't want me there. I didn't understand why.

But the children were beautiful and stronger than they were. I asked them to draw about their Christmas holiday and they taped their voices as they were telling the story of their drawings. We had a very good time. The film is called "Christmas at Moose Factory".

Following that experience, I devoted a lot of time to creating educational, audio-visual materials. It should be mentioned that those persons interested in these projects took part in the production work; also that the materials were first produced in the language of the tribe concerned, and later versioned into English and French.

The government departments paying for this type of production got upset because it was costly and took a long, long time. Maybe eventually they will realize and understand the value of these programs.

Sometimes when I sing in a small town close to a reserve, I bring an old person up on the stage with me. Although this person has been a neighbour all his life, the children are very disturbed at first because most probably they had been taught to have prejudices towards that old person. Maybe because of the way he dresses, his drinking habits or the fact that he is an Indian.

After a while, as he is telling them stories and singing, the children always fall in love with this person. This is to say that judgments are made on people all the time. One forgets that a person is many things and to want to give is the most important one.

This is why I have spent so much of my time at the National Film Board because I have found a new way to communicate with children and people all over the world.

Marjorie Perley

Marjorie Perley, a Maliseet Indian, was born in 1934 on the Tobique reserve in New Brunswick where she now lives. Even though they moved off the reserve when she was only five, her parents always spoke Maliseet at home. When she found out that the language was declining among the 600 Maliseets on her reserve, Marjorie devised a writing system, compiled a dictionary and taught oral classes for four years at the reserve school. Marjorie's dictionary is not being used at the moment because there has not yet been any official recognition of a Maliseet writing style. She encourages all efforts to preserve her culture. She formed a group of dancers, planned Indian celebrations in 1967 and more recently organized the New Brunswick Council of Native Women.

Not growing up on the reserve, I fully appreciated the homey atmosphere when I did move back. My earliest

recollection was hearing my father saying the rosary in Maliseet. During the winter months he would tell us stories after we were all in bed. Back then it was not uncommon for whole families to sleep in one room and it's too bad that families today do not have this kind of closeness. Since my own children started coming, I was really concerned about them missing out on some of the greatest things in life that our parents gave us such as the many legends and stories, especially ghost stories, of the Maliseets. I didn't want them to hang their heads because they were Indians, simply from lack of knowledge. I sort of looked around for a way to revive some of it. In 1956, I organized the Tobique dancers. Not knowing very much about our culture or dances I found what I could in written and oral history, put it in dance form and then taught it to the young people. This is when I first noticed the loss of our language. When I instructed in Maliseet I found that the young people could not understand quite a bit of what I said. Only about 70 per cent of the older generation on our reserve use it and only to each other, not to their children or grandchildren. In my opinion, home is the most important place to start.

With encouragement of the New Brunswick Human Rights Commission, I obtained a grant to look into the possibility of devising a writing system and preparing a primer in Maliseet. It is not a written language and I found using phonetics too difficult. When I put myself in the place of a student I thought, since we already know the English alphabet, there must be some way we could use that to get as close to the sounds as possible. I worked

107 with a professor at the University of New Brunswick and two Maliseets. Meanwhile I received a Ford Foundation grant for what I really wanted to do – research into the Algonquin culture and to familiarize myself with the languages to give me a deeper insight into the sounds for comparison purposes. This took me a year so I sort of let go of the first grant. Then I was hired to work with 18 high school dropouts to find a method of teaching native languages and I worked with a graduate from the Massachusetts Institute of Technology. I was really on a linguistic kick so in the fall of 1970 I went to MIT, in Cambridge, Mass., as a special student and assistant to a professor studying grammatical complexities in North American Indian languages.

Later that fall, I lost my oldest son in a car accident and it took me some time to get a hold of myself, so I left MIT and got a job at the reserve school teaching Maliseet to primary grades. I tried to work closely with the teachers to find out what the children were studying in English. For a start I taught them to count to ten in Maliseet and wrote a song to make it easier for them. Then we learned the days of the week, months, and casual conversation. Here I found the writing system came in handy. When I went into the school I had nothing, and I mean nothing, no materials or prepared lessons. Some of the parents told me they were learning from their children and asked me if I would hold evening classes. One of them thanked me very much for all that I have taught his children. I don't think any teacher could ask for a greater reward.

Millie Redmond

Millie Redmond, a Pottawatomi Indian from Walpole Island, lost her parents when she was four years old. In the 11 years she spent in an orphanage she learned a lot which helped in her work with Indian people in Toronto. Millie started a social club that grew into the Friendship Centre and she is now director of Anduhyan, a home for young native women.

When I was growing up my ambition was to be able to support myself and not rely on welfare. I have some happy memories about the orphanage but having been raised by non-Indians, I wanted to know more native history about my past and get involved with my own people. That was 25 years ago and I didn't realize just how fully I would get involved. Now, when I'm home, I have to remind myself that I need to work at keeping my home intact too. My husband is very understanding. He just says, "We'll see you when you come home," which makes me feel warm and happy inside.

When I first came to Toronto to work in an office, I didn't know any Indian people. Then as I gradually got to know some I decided we needed a club, so I called the "Y" and asked if we could use their facilities. Our big project was to visit Indian and Inuit people in hospital and take them candy, cookies and comics. Thirteen years after, when the Friendship Centre was formed, I was asked to work full-time and eventually became director.

For about six years before that I was working in court and learned a lot from the other workers and native people who had been there a long time. Sometimes I would be afraid to get up in front of a certain judge and one of them would nudge me and say, "Go on."

It was early in 1974 that I was chosen Citizen of the Month by Toronto Metro Citizenship Committee.

The Board from Anduhyan asked me to take over Anduhyan. In Ojibway it means "our home" and it's the only place in the city for native girls – a sort of home away from home. The girls stay here anywhere from a week to six months. The average is three or four months. It was started by the YWCA and funded by the Department of Indian and Northern Affairs, as a home for girls who came to the city to go to school because most of them wanted to go back to their reserves. The girls here now don't want to go home – they've left home. Unfortunately some of them haven't enough education to get jobs and we try to steer some of them back home or to school or work. The whole thing about living here is that the girls realize it is a home where they can get involved in helping each other and where they can know there is pleasure in giv-

109 ing, and pleasure in living, and by just helping each other they can have a world that is a little different.

People used to say you mustn't mingle the good girls with the bad girls, but who knows who is a good girl. Tell me, who knows? As far as I'm concerned they are all good. So we try to deal with them as individuals. The rules are not hard. We try to instill a bit of responsibility to the house, the community and themselves. I think we accomplish more than we realize because after the girls have left, they come back just for a visit. This gives them a feeling that they're meeting their own friends, young mothers helping each other. There's a warmth here. Most of the girls are young but we do have older women sometimes arrive through welfare, churches and institutions, from the Indian Centre or from the Department of Indian and Northern Affairs. It seems, lately, that we are getting involved more in the correctional field.

When they come into the cities they find values are quite a bit different to what they knew. They spend money like crazy and don't know where it is gone. They have to learn about paying rent and how to survive – so much to learn. The other thing is loneliness. Here we teach them pottery and native crafts and give them counselling on health and child care. No one does anything free. They all get paid for their fabulous beadwork and for their help around the place. It's a learning experience for them. I would love to see young boys here too. We could put them up on the top floor when we get a fire-escape and they too could be part of the family. But that's another bag of beans.

Sarah Sark

Island abandoned for 35 years. Sarah is a member of the Advisory Council on the Status of Women and a member of the Native Women's Association of Canada.

When I left school I worked for a doctor, then later I went to work in a hospital. I assisted anybody that needed help; doctors, nurses and people working in the lab, X-ray department or the wards. Nothing is easy in a hospital. It is a very difficult place to work but once you get used to it and it gets in your blood, it's the kind of life you want. I still wonder why I left. For a time I worked on the E.E.G. machine – that's the one that measures brain waves. I liked it. Not too many people do that work and I would have loved to learn more about it but my supervisor made me move and I meekly went back and did the job I was doing. I'm timid and shy and if anybody says anything offensive to me, I don't answer back. But if that happened to me today, I would have said, "To heck with you, I want to learn this." Working in a hospital is very rewarding. When you look back you feel you have contributed something.

After being away from Canada my husband wanted to come home, so we moved down here and started the reserve. When we first came this place was a dump. It was abandoned for 35 years and there was just nothing here. We were one of three families who got together and made plans for clearing the land. We decided what we were all going to do and everybody was given a job to do, including the children. My husband and two daughters built this house. We had no power so everything was done by hand.

Sarah Sark, a Micmac woman born in St. Peter's, Nova Scotia, was one of 14 children. When her parents died, she left school after grade ten and supported the family for eight years. After living some time in the United States she and her husband and two children moved to Rocky Point, a reserve on Prince Edward

111   We didn't get power until later on that year. We fixed our own lots, landscaping them ourselves. I'm telling you, all you need is plenty of elbow grease and determination.

We're three-quarters of a mile from the main road and we wanted to pave the road to the reserve, so a neighbour coordinated a walkathon, 17 miles to Charlottetown, to raise funds. Everybody took part, people who have cottages near here, neighbours around, a priest and a nun, some children came from Charlottetown – we didn't even know who they were. Two six-year-olds made it all the way. We got some help from the provincial government, material like grading and stuff for the road, and we had a LIP program and we built a community centre which is used for kids' dances and social gatherings and meetings.

There's a lot native people can do to help themselves. To me, education is the most important thing. I would like to see my children finish their education. Without it, you can't get anywhere. I felt very proud at the time I was asked to sit on the Advisory Council on the Status of Women and I would like to see more Indian women taking part in other areas, maybe the Women's Council of Canada and these various organizations, and be involved in government programs. Indian people are sometimes not aware what's going on and decisions are made without them being consulted. If anybody sits on the board then they'll know what's going on. I'll do my best to do the job right and expect to help native women any way I can but I have lots to learn. I can't do it overnight. I don't know what's going to happen tomorrow and neither do you.

Monica Turner

Born into a very poor Ojibway family near Nipigon in northern Ontario, Monica Turner had little chance of formal education but was brought up with a sense of pride in her Indianness. She now lives in Thunder Bay. During the 1930's, her grandfather, Chief Joe Sault, was one of the greatest promoters of Indian culture and she learned from him to work unselfishly for what she believed in. Monica has spent much time and energy in voluntary work and the executive positions she has held are too numerous to list. Among other things she has been on the Board of Directors of the Union of Ontario Indians, vice-chairman of the National Association of Friendship Centres, a member of the first steering committee of the Native Women's Association of Canada and national coordinator of Indian Rights for Indian Women. In spite of all that, her Cree husband and eight children know they come first. They are her life.

My grandfather was a great influence on me. Sometimes when I would go home from school crying because I felt I didn't have a friend, he would say, "Stand proud for you are an Indian. Stand as proud as you can and if they call you names just stretch a bit taller and tell them I am proud of what I am. We are not foreigners in this country. This is our country and don't forget that." He used to talk about the downfall of our people and would say, "Don't ever let yourself go to the bottle." Even in those days drinking was quite a problem. He told me the best thing to go on in life is to try and figure out for yourself, try and distinguish to yourself what is right and what is wrong and never let yourself down.

I have to admit that we have this feeling of inferiority. You're not born with it. It kind of is built around you. I didn't have it until I went to school. Then I realized that I was sort of different. I found it very hard. There is definitely discrimination. When I went into a store they'd come right away where I was and stand beside me, not because they wanted to help but keeping track that I did not snitch anything. That's the kind of thing that hurts.

I like to believe that society is changing. I never look down on anybody. I don't care who he is. I always treat them equally but some native people can really be mean. When I moved to a new town and I first talked to them they seemed fairly friendly, but they drank quite a bit and resented me. I took a lot of ridicule. When I walked down the street they would talk in Indian and call me dirty names. It was a sort of jealousy and that's the way it is with many Indian people. Everybody thinks that we are crying unity but we're so far from it that it's pathetic.

I have belonged to many native organizations, all in good faith, and have given up a lot of my valuable time because it is something I believe in. Because I've been downtrodden and humiliated I thought maybe I could help. I think with Indian people generally it all starts out that way. But now people have gone off the track somewhere along the way and are working for their personal gain. We're going to have to take a realistic look at what we're doing and not let our personal interests get the best of us as that is detrimental to what we've already done. It saddens me but it's no use pretending it doesn't happen – people use people to get ahead. And when you feel you're

113 being used rather than helping, where do you go? People will say, "If you believe in what you really say you believe in, why did you give up?"

A lot of awareness has been created in society which is a very good thing as society needs to be changed for its own sake. The sad part of it is that attitudes to government grants for native organizations will be, "Why should we give the Indian people something?" Even Indian politicians say they're afraid to let Indian women have their status because of the cost but I can't see that there would be a stampede going to the reserves. Now that native women have a voice, it should be heard. This shouldn't be spoiled. It should be held in great respect. Becoming united to regain our status which was lost through legislation, that's very important. Being treaty is not important but having your status is. After living half of my life as an Indian person there's no way they're going to change my mind. I know I'm an Indian, but it is important to me that it's documented. I think that government should change that piece of legislation and give us our status.

I became involved in native organizations around 1954. Then there was so much hope in what could be done. Maybe I was naive and living in a dream-type world which doesn't exist but I think everyone did things with their hearts and did a lot of negotiating. It was a growing period. A lot of good things happened. Then bureaucracy got into the picture and now people who run organizations run them solely for the purpose of their livelihood, which is really bad. That's where white politics is – it's no use pretending it doesn't happen. They talk about grass-roots level but I know from experience there's no such thing as communication with people at the grass-roots level. It saddens me to see selfish motives crumble the good. That's life, I suppose, but it shouldn't be that way. My people have learned it.

Inuit

115

Nellie Cournoyea

Nellie Cournoyea was born in Aklavik, in the Mackenzie delta, *in 1940. For some years she has been a spokesman for the Committee for Original Peoples' Entitlement (COPE) and is now on a year's leave from her job as manager of the CBC radio station in Inuvik to work with a land claims negotiating committee in the western region.*

Communication is one of the big problems in the north. From the beginning, COPE's role was to explain to the people that times are changing and to bring them a knowledge of what was going on in the north because very little information, still, is getting to the people. It seems to me that a lot of people are basing their talk on what can happen and what might happen, but there are lots of things that are happening already.

Industrial development is going to come. There's no point in debating it. It's too late. In Inuvik there are three hotels and they are all booked up and now there are plans for major development of a trailer park to accommodate 300 trailers. There are champagne tours coming in with people from Wall Street and major magazines. Economic power is at the bottom of everything. The native people need help – right now. They know what the problems are but they need scientific backup. People are too often presented with only one idea rather than seeing different alternatives.

I can tell you some of the problems. I travel to settlements quite often and get a good view of activities. There's a lack of follow-up concerning complaints made by people. For instance there are streams that haven't

117 been cleaned up by oil companies and when you go back to them and say there is damage, they say, "I don't see any damage," or "It won't happen again." Native people need a forum to express themselves. They have proved that they know what needs to be done. What they need is to be educated with information so they know what alternatives there are. Native people in the Northwest Territories are normally very trustful people – until recently when we found that our trust has been abused. There are 28,500 native peoples in Northwest Territories and I don't believe that, if you consider the land usage, the population should be increased any degree. I would say that each family should have 3,000 square miles to survive. This includes caribou hunting and the use of water. The land belongs to the people.

Fifteen years ago in the western Arctic, there was very little welfare. People looked after themselves and we seemed to get along quite well. There were people who died too but there are two kinds of death – one is a mental one and one is a physical one. Our people now are dying mentally because there isn't equality. We are willing to make changes, to adapt two different ways of life together to make a very good one, solving the problems of making us mobile and making our decisions by ourselves. Native people need help and information so they know what alternatives are possible. Paternalism has been a failure.

Ann Pilitak Hanson

Ann Pilitak Hanson was born in Lake Harbour, Northwest Territories, in 1946. Her father died when she was four and a few years later her mother caught tuberculosis and died in a hospital in the south. Ann lives in Apex, a settlement three miles from Frobisher Bay. She is active in community affairs and was asked to be Frobisher's first Justice of the Peace but refused for personal reasons. Recently she acted in a film about Arctic life, "White Dawn."

I never got to know my mother or father and was brought up back and forth by aunts and uncles. In 1957, we travelled to Frobisher Bay by boat. That was the year I started school. When we went to school we had to have an interpreter. Frobisher kids spoke English already so they were interpreting for us. They had been in school for two years. We had one teacher and were a class of young ones and old ones. I was the oldest, about 10 or 11. It was very embarrassing. I guess we envied the kids who spoke English. I found school very dull and tried to quit at grade five but the teacher came after me and said, "You stay in school until you finish."

When I was 13 or 14 I went to live in Toronto but was very homesick and wanted to go back up north after I finished school. The people I was living with said, "If you went to secretarial school, you'd be through in one year then could go back and work there." So I did, then I came back to Frobisher and was very happy. There was a job with the CBC here and I became secretary, announcer-operator and worked to produce and direct a lot of Inuit programs. That was very interesting. Then I met my husband and now I have four daughters.

There are more Inuit women active in community affairs than men. Probably because we talk more, we complain more, and by complaining you're going to be heard and then the problem can be worked out when it's brought into the open. Men are very quiet here in the north, they seem to be waiting for somebody else to do it. The woman is always the boss of the house but, once they get out on the land, the men take over and the woman needs the man. Now the women have to work to survive, go out and look for jobs, and there are not that many jobs in the north for women or anybody.

The worst change I have seen is the very fast taking over of the north by the south. Suddenly in Frobisher there are more white people than Inuit. The people from the south have jobs, nice homes, holidays. I've been trying to find a way to slow down the taking over of the community in some way that lets local people control how many people come from the south in a year. I feel there are many jobs that the Inuit can have here which are held by whites. I'm not racist or anything. I have concern for the Inuit who are going to be living here the rest of their lives.

One of the things I am very bitter about is we can't build our own homes. We can't get land. There is no question who owns the land. We know from way, way back the land belongs to the Inuit but when any person

119 wants to build, the government says, "No." In 1954, when the people were living in camps, the government came to them and asked, "Where would you like to live around Frobisher Bay?" So the people had a meeting, all the hunters, and they agreed to this location. It was beautiful, lots of fresh running water from the lake, so they built the village of Apex for Inuit and all the people who had agreed to live here signed a paper and that letter was sent to Ottawa. But now the government wants to close Apex down. We had a general meeting and people don't plan to move out because this is their home. Just over 100 people live here. It's got a school and a dock – that's where all the Frobisher people dump all their garbage. But we live here instead of there because it is so much nicer.

I always feel sad when people talk about Frobisher as being an alcohol problem area. I know there are really heavy drinking people and they are the ones who keep coming back to court and, when they come back so many times, people think, "Gee, everybody in Frobisher drinks." It's not that way. There are lots of people here who don't drink at all.

If I was Prime Minister, I would like to find out what people would really like to do and what kind of jobs they would like to have. I'd make the training available in northern communities, not send people south.

The best job I ever had was acting in the film "White Dawn" because we were together all the time, a lot of Inuit. The film crew was friendly and very human but the best part was I was with my own people and outdoors most of the time. It was very exciting.

Monica Ittuksarjuag

Monica Ittuksarjuag was born in 1951 near Arctic Bay at the north end of Baffin Island. She is the great-granddaughter of a strong leader in a community of hunters who suffered terrible hardships from sickness and starvation, and Monica has done some hunting with her own family. She is now married with three children and lives in Igloolik where she hopes to start a local newspaper.

My oldest child was born the month I was supposed to go to Fort Smith to a teacher's education program and I had a letter from the government saying there was absolutely no accommodation for married couples with children, so we decided that my mother-in-law should take care of the baby. When we realized the child would become attached to my mother-in-law, we decided to have her adopt it. My family is eight altogether. I have three real brothers and mother adopted two boys and two girls. I stayed a year and a half in Fort Smith but did not finish the course. We took a lot of theory courses in teaching methods but things I learned didn't turn out in practice. I moved around for a while and worked in day-care centres. Then I was assistant teacher in a school in Frobisher Bay and later became assistant to the adult educator there. My husband has now gone to Fort Smith to get educated in heavy-duty mechanics so I came here to Igloolik and stayed and helped with the adult educators. I like it very much.

My husband goes out hunting when he is here. We used to live in the traditional way. A couple of years ago we went out caribou hunting in summer time with my in-laws. First we put everything on the boat and went to a camp to sleep. We pitched up our tent and had to carry all our provisions up to it, then go and fetch some water. It went like this until we got to our destination where there was caribou. I walked with my husband looking for caribou. We had to walk miles and miles until we shot some, then carry all the meat back to the tent. In camp we feasted and dried up some meat, prepared the caribou skin for clothing and so on. Also we gathered moss for a fire and did some cooking. Once, in winter, we went out to go seal hunting but we didn't catch any seals. It wasn't much fun sleeping out in the open. It was cold. In the old days, when

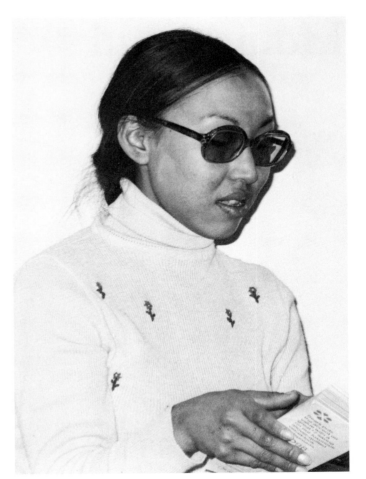

121 one person caught some meat we would call everybody and give some meat free, but nowadays most of the hunters sell their catch to the co-op and if we want some meat we have to buy it. We need money to survive and that is one change I don't really like.

In Igloolik some women are really independent and progressive but others are just talking and not doing anything. I like to consider myself one of the active ones but there are times when I get discouraged and just drop everything. We're trying to get the people to do something about day-care centres right now. They're trying to raise some money, but the president of the committee is a man. I think it should be a woman. I don't think people know much about day-care centres and how they operate. Some men are suggesting how to take care of kids when they don't care for the kids themselves. There are so many kids in Igloolik and no birth control. People are against it for religious reasons mostly and health reasons. My cousin and I have been thinking of starting a newspaper here but there is no money for it. We want to do it voluntarily.

People would like to have a newspaper, I know a whole lot of people who do, but they won't support you unless you start it and we haven't started it yet. There is so little communication in this town. Right now, people go around and talk behind people's backs. I think if there was a newspaper, people here would read other people's opinions, find out what is going on and write about their grievances. Then the person in charge would hear about it and do something.

Lydia Maliki

Lydia Maliki was born in Igloolik and now, in her mid-thirties, lives 60 miles south of there in Hall Beach, a community of about 150 people. She did not go to school and speaks very little English. After a visit to Toronto for a craft workshop for Arctic women, Lydia organized a program teaching crafts in Hall Beach to women who hope to sell their work. She has three children.

There were ten in my family, the same number of boys as girls. My mother died when I was 12 years old and I couldn't do anything. I met loneliness and hunger and ever since that time I used to think that, when I got older, I want to help the poor, the hungry, the orphans. I used to think that a lot. I remember a long time ago when my mother was alive and I was small, when parents died the orphans wouldn't have so much clothing and someone would have to make clothes for them. Now when there are orphans, everything – parkas, rubber boots – can be bought. A long time ago, men were hunting more to get food for their families but now most of them are working at jobs so we don't have as much native food to eat. I miss it very much. In springtime I go fishing. I haven't been hunting seals since 1959. I loved to go hunting and wait until the seals came home, then shoot them. Some men used harpoons but I used to shoot. Just when the seal comes up you shoot but you have to be pretty quick to catch it before it goes down.

I was in the south in a sanitorium for one year. What I didn't like most was the food. I used to throw up sometimes at meals. I was very happy to get back north. I never went to school but for a month I was taking a course in English before I went to Toronto to a conference. Before that I was thinking about how to get women to work and do something to make money for themselves but I didn't know how to get it started. I thought I could buy all the material myself and give it to a person who doesn't have enough money and tell them to make something, like a duffle sack or something, so that she could sell it and get

123   money. I wanted to help the women who were widowed or poor, to start them so they could do something to earn money. In other settlements they have a sewing centre where the women get together. I wanted to start things like weaving and macrame. I asked the ladies here whether they would like something like this. In Toronto I was given an address to write to when we were ready to start, so I wrote. I was thinking that I would still keep my job and the ladies could work by themselves, but they wanted me to be the teacher.

There are 17 women working with me, mostly old, that is, over 20 years old. I don't like to have too many young ones because they don't know how to do native work like making parkas and if they come to this class they might not learn their own traditions. In school they have started to teach Inuit sewing. I would like to see young girls be like us older people, able to start what we are doing. My husband was very pleased and wanted to buy things I make. We plan to sell to the co-op or to the men working at the base who are down from the south. We work three hours for five days a week. Half the women go to the course in the morning and the other half in the afternoon. Those who don't have babysitters take their children along. The ladies seem to enjoy it very much. They haven't seen this kind of work before. They just started and they're very good.

Pitseolalak Kelly

Pitseolalak Kelly does not know her age but remembers living with her family, somewhere on Baffin Island, in igloos and seal skin tents, moving from camp to camp when her father was hunting. Her early memories are of how hard her mother worked and of seeing white people for the first time. Now she lives in Frobisher Bay and is president of the senior citizens group. Pitseolalak had ten children, only four of whom are still living.

My first memory is the time we went to the settlement where they had white people. It was the first time I had playmates besides my sister. I enjoyed it and didn't want to leave. We were waiting for a ship travelling to Cape Dorset. My father was needed to work to develop the

Hudson's Bay store. After it was built we moved out and lived in camps and my father was trapping for the trading post. He was a very good hunter and saw we had enough food and clothing. I used to wonder why mother was giving away our clothing but found out that she was helping the people who didn't have too much.

My mother was a very busy woman, she never seemed to finish working. I remember how busy she was during every season change, making clothing, coats, pants, even boots. Before the winter they were made out of caribou skin and when spring was coming it was all sealskin. She would get up early in the morning, sewing all day, even during the late evenings. She was always ready to help her husband. Early in the morning she would help him to harness the dogs and when he came home she would help him until he was finished, even though she had other things to do. The women never seemed to get tired or even sick. They were always busy.

Our parents trained us very well at an early age even though we thought it was not time to know these things. My mother told us always to be prepared for our own families, never to be lazy and always to be ready for different seasons. We were very obedient. A girl used to get married when the parents thought she was old enough to make clothing and manage by herself to have a husband. Even when I got married and had children, the Inuit never stayed in settlements all the time. They would spend summers there but would rather live in their camps in winter. I helped many women who had to give birth and I did many things whenever I was asked. Even now I

125 am getting old, others ask me to do something and I am willing to help. That's the way I am brought up. If I can do it, I never refuse. Most things I do today are making parkas and boots. They need chewing to soften them before the sewing and my teeth are not that new any more. I hardly have any teeth. I hardly do any good sewing now because I need glasses. Pretty soon I won't be able to do it any more.

Our senior citizens club is mainly for old people who live alone, so they are able to get together as companions. It has really helped us as friends to have something to do and it makes us happier. We long to see each other. We do some sewing, like making parkas, to make something for someone, but I told them this place was for us to have fun, to enjoy ourselves and to do whatever we wish to do in our own way. We meet three times a week from 1:00 pm to 5:00 pm. When we first started we were going every day, but it was too much because we have something else to do at home too.

Young people today, they don't live the way we were and it's sad to see they are losing the Inuit ways. My daughter helps me around the house. Other women complain about their daughters. They don't help and I think it is a sad thing.

Nowadays everything is happening in English. It's a great help to school children to learn English but when you think about it seriously, there aren't many young people who speak Inuktituk. When talking to them strictly in Inuktituk, they won't understand you and I would ask them, "How can't you."

Design:
Eiko Emori

Photography Credits:
Edith Dahlschen: pp. 13, 15, 17, 23, 25, 35, 37,
                  39, 43, 47, 51, 53, 55, 57,
                  63, 67, 71, 77, 79, 83, 85,
                  87, 89, 93, 95, 97, 99, 101,
                  103, 107, 109, 111

Philip Hersee: p. 19
Stephen Kendall: pp. 21, 27
Hans Heinrich Heinsohn: p. 25
Murray Mosher: p. 29
Terry Bland: p. 33
Henry Kalen: pp. 45, 49
Jim Parker: p. 61
Sam Corrigan: p. 75
Ed Kucerak: p. 105
Denis Hill: p. 113

Tsimshian mask made by Freda Deising: p. 11
Cree Beaded Draw Purse made by Freda Wesaquate: p. 41
Métis Carved Whale Bone made
   by Lorraine Bronson: p. 59
Mohawk Ceramic Teapot made by Sylvia Smith: p. 81
Algonquin Woman Scraping Hide drawn
   by Daphne Odjig: p. 91